WA in
SOUTH LA LAND
Book 2

Based on
Walks in the Kendal Area
Series 3 2nd Edition
It was decided to change the title of this book
as the walks spread over quite a wide area.

Published by

**the Kendal Group
of the
Ramblers' Association**

June 2009

ISBN: 978-1-906494-13-1

Also in this series
Walks in the Kendal Area Book 1 (3rd edition)
Walks in South Lakeland

The name, address and telephone number of the current
Secretary of the Kendal group can be obtained from Kendal Library
or Kendal Tourist Information Centre

The first editions of these booklets were researched and complied
by Margaret Adams.

Key map for the location of walks

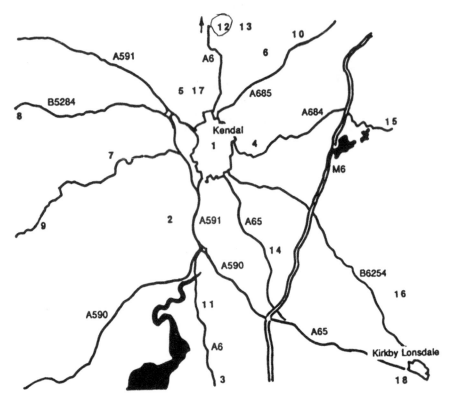

Key to Map Starting Points

Editor   Tim Baynes
Maps revised   Peter Standish
Photographs   Bryan Harris, Tim Baynes and Michael Squires
Cover photograph   Longsleddale - the track up to Gatescarth

All the texts were reviewed and checked by members of the Kendal Ramblers Group.

Maps based on O S 1:25,000 under licence from Ordnance Survey

Index

Arranged in order of length of walk

Shorter options in brackets

Although the descriptions and sketch maps are intended to give you all the guidance you need to follow these walks, we recommend that you take the 1:25,000 Ordnance Survey maps with you, as they may help, if the text or the diagrams are not quite clear.

One of the aims of the Ramblers is to preserve Public Rights of Way. We hope that by publishing this series of Books of Walks, people may be encouraged to use the network of paths in South Lakeland and therefore keep them open and well used.

Chapel Beck, Chapel House, near Underbarrow

A beck typifies South Lakeland
A finger post tells you it is a Right of Way
A stile suggests new possibilities on the other side

WALK NO. 1
The Town of Kendal   6.5km (4 miles)

This route will give walkers a general idea of the topography of Kendal. There are some steep climbs, but they are worth it as they provide some excellent views of the surrounding countryside. The walk is an introduction to the history and architecture of the town. Plaques at key points mounted by the Kendal Civic Society are helpful and there are many relevant publications available at the Town Hall Information Office. An up to date street plan, which could be useful, is also available from there.

Start
At the wrought iron gates in front of the Parish Church, at the south end of the main street, cross the road and look for a very narrow ginnel signed Kirkbarrow Lane, known locally as t'Crack, next to the Wheatsheaf Inn.

Looking North East you will catch a glimpse, in winter, of Castle Howe, which you will visit shortly. At the end, turn right and cross over into Buttery Well Road.

Continue with the children's playground on your left. Go straight over the next crossroads to reach Gillingate through bollards. The route continues across the road as Buttery Well Lane, to reach Captain French Lane.

Turn left and almost immediately right up Garth Heads, a steep walled path or ginnel. After about 50m go up the steep steps on the left. The steps lead to the open green of Bowling Fell, with the motte and bailey Castle Howe beyond. This is the earlier and less well known of Kendal's two castles. The motte is surmounted by an obelisk erected in 1788 to commemorate the centenary of the 1688 Revolution leading to the abdication of James II.

Having explored Bowling Fell, find a walled path in its North West corner (by an electricity pole) leading between houses to Beast Banks, a very old part of Kendal where animals were once baited before slaughter and butchery. Turn right down the steep hill, and cross the road to follow the pavement round to the left into Low Fellside, which marks the eastern boundary of Fellside, once a notorious slum area, now redeveloped and modernised, but retaining many of the old ginnels and steps.

Immediate on the left climb up the cobbled Sepulchre Lane, passing an old Quaker burial ground on the left. Pass Cliff Brow and Church Terrace and go up the steep steps on the left to reach the junction of Serpentine Road and Queens Road. Cross over Queens Road and enter Serpentine Woods by the path to the left of Serpentine Cottage. Keep bearing right at the path junctions, to go alongside a small tree nursery, gradually climbing through the woods. When you reach a path coming in from the left turn right and then immediately left.

You will soon emerge through a wide gap in a wall just below Kendal Golf Course. From here there is a wide view of the upper Kent valley, the eastern Lakeland fells and the skyline round to the Howgill fells, with Kendal and Benson Knott in the foreground. Go about 100m along a well trodden path over this flat open space and then aim slightly right and downhill towards a clump of mature beech and pine trees.

Drop steeply down to a track running alongside a wall. Find a squeeze stile in the wall just below the trees, leading into the corner of a field. Through the stile, go diagonally across the field downhill, aiming for the trees in the corner, above the allotments. Pass through the small gate on top of the stile near the trees and turn right, passing the remains of an old barn. Go through a gateway on the right to join a path down beside the wall. When you reach some locked iron gates at the bottom of this path, go through a stile and small metal gate in the wall on the right and follow the track down to Windermere Road.

Turn left, then cross the busy road with great care into Fairfield Lane opposite. This gives access to Kendal Green, a large open space. Cross the green diagonally to the right to a cross roads. Go down Horncop Lane. In about 150m find a footpath sign on the right, which gives access to a path down to Ashleigh Road. Follow the road to the right, to its junction with Burneside Road.

Go left along Burneside Road, then turn first right, down Dockray Hall Road. Bear slightly right to reach the River Kent. Follow the river downstream to Victoria Bridge, crossing the road there by a pedestrian crossing and continuing on the same bank to Stramongate Bridge. Now go left, over the bridge into Wildman Street. Use the pedestrian crossing and turn left, noting in passing the Castle Dairy opposite, Kendal's oldest house. This dates from at least the 14th Century.

Gates, Parish Church, Kendal

At the major road junction turn right into Ann Street. At the far end turn left into Castle Street, and then in 200m take the second right into Castle Road. (Kendal's oldest municipal cemetery is on the right.

About 100m up Castle Road is a footpath sign to Kendal Castle on the right. Go through the kissing gate and then up a gravel track and the long shoulder of the hill to the castle. This is later and better known than Castle Howe. Some historians believe it has associations with Katherine Parr, the last and surviving wife of Henry VIII.

The drumlin, on which it stands was carved by a glacier during one of the ice ages. Here you have a second main view point of the walk. Looking West across Kendal there is Scout Scar. To the North there is the Whinfell range and to the east Benson Knott.

After exploring the castle ruins follow the path a short way round the embankment (anticlockwise) on the town side and descend by a grassy path and steep steps to a kissing gate leading to Sunnyside, with Fletcher Park on the left. Continue down the road, over the bridge which crosses the former Lancaster canal (now a cycle route). On reaching the main road use the pedestrian crossing on your right and take the footbridge over the Kent.

After crossing this turn left along the river. Turn right just before Abbott Hall Art Gallery, then left with the museum of Lakeland Life and Industry on your right. The Parish Church is ahead. Turn right to the start of the walk.

WALK No. 2
Scout Scar from Helsington Church
7.2km (4.5miles)   300ft of climb

St John's Church, Helsington is the Parish Church of Brigsteer and is remarkable for its isolated position on the edge of the limestone escarpment overlooking the Lyth Valley. The views to the Lakeland Fells and Morecambe Bay are magnificent. The Wheatsheaf Inn at Brigsteer, the village visited on the walk, is a good stopping place if refreshments are required.

Drive about 3 miles South West of Kendal on the road to Brigsteer.
Turn left immediately before the road starts to descend the escarpment. Go along to Helsington church. There is room for parking in front of the church except during Sunday services. Grid reference SD 488892.

OS map 1:25:000 OL7 North Sheet

Start
Walk back along the track to the road, and then go uphill for a short distance to the footpath sign on the left pointing to Scout Scar. Follow the broad grassy track to the gate at the end of the National Trust land, and continue through the gate until the track turns sharp right and descends into a small valley.

Climb steeply out of the small valley and take the track through a wide gap in the end wall onto the open fellside. Walk for 700m along Scout Scar. At a large cairn, opposite the farm below, a path descends the scar steeply through woods.

1. Cross the field towards Barrowfield Farm on the cart track beside the wall on your right, and follow the waymarked route to the left of the farm buildings.

>   (You could take a short cut on reaching the farm drive, to shorten the walk considerably - see map).

On reaching the farm drive turn right then follow the sign pointing left in front of the farmhouse, going downhill and into the wood by a stile. After going through the wood, cross a field to another stile and enter a plantation.

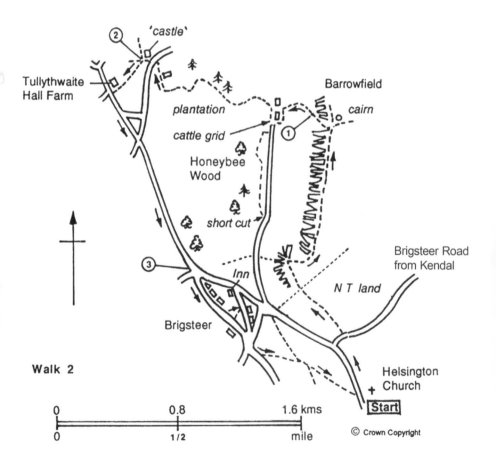

8

Follow the path straight ahead through the plantation, ignoring all cross-paths, until you reach a forestry road. Turn right then left after 30m to follow roughly the line of the overhead power lines until the path descends via a left and right turn to reach a gate into a field. Cross the field to the left of the house, skirting around the old orchard to reach a track going right, to join the house drive. On reaching the road turn left for about 40m and go through the first field gate on the right, entering a field near a small barn, locally known as 'the Castle', a clue to its probable history.

2. Follow the track by the wall and go through a gate on the left (ignoring the wall stile ahead). Follow the track that descends to the left of the farm buildings at Tullythwaite Hall and emerge onto the road by a stile. Turn left along the road for 1.75km.

3. When you reach a four way junction at the edge of Brigsteer village go straight ahead onto the minor road. Follow this for about 170m to a narrow path on the left, that starts opposite the first house on the right   The walled path leads steeply up left to another road.

Along this road to the left is the Wheatsheaf Inn, which serves bar meals, etc. but the walk continues to the right. Follow the road through the village, ignoring all side roads, until near the end of the village you reach a footpath sign to St John's Church on the left. Follow the path up to a gated stile, then bear diagonally right uphill and along a new fence to a waymarked stile. Continue up the next field to a stile leading onto an unmetalled track. Turn right along the track and after about 120m look for a steep and narrow path slanting up through the wood on the left. This leads via a stile to the open fell below Helsington Church, which you'll soon see among the trees on the skyline.

WALK NO. 3

Beetham, Slackhead and the Fairy Steps
7.2km (4.5miles)   About 300ft of climb

This is mainly a woodland walk, exploring part of the Arnside and Silverdale which is designated an Area of Outstanding Natural Beauty.

9 miles South of Kendal on the A6 the walk starts from the historic village of Beetham with its ancient church and working watermill, the route passes the medieval pele tower of Beetham Hall, crosses some rare limestone pavements

and visits the famous 'Fairy Steps'. The limestone can be very slippery if wet.

Drive past the first turn into Beetham. About 200m further on turn right into the second turning. Park along this road. (SD 497795).

OS map 1:25,000 OL7 South Sheet.

Start
Look for the telephone kiosk. Follow the signpost pointing to Hale. The path goes beside a house to a gate leading into a field. Head diagonally across the field half left, to reach a stone squeeze stile in the corner above Beetham Hall and its medieval pele tower. Go along the bottom of the wood to another stile.

Continue just outside the wood and below the outcrops, to reach a short enclosed lane leading out of the corner of the field. Ignore the stile and weathered finger post directly ahead. Instead follow the rising enclosed lane to another stile.

Continue to, and then follow the sign to Slackhead along the Limestone Link Path, (a 15mile route between Arnside and Kirkby Lonsdale). After a few

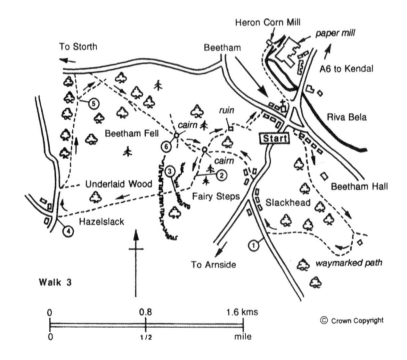

metres go straight ahead at the cross paths. The path goes uphill through the woods. Look out for closely spaced yellow waymarks over the next 800metres, particularly for the transition marker from woodland path to limestone pavement. This is a rare and protected habitat for a variety of plants growing in the 'grykes' between the `clints'. Care is needed in crossing this, especially when the rock is wet

1.   On reaching the road turn right and follow it for 500m, past a junction on the left, to a signpost on the left pointing to Storth and the Fairy Steps. Still on the Limestone Link path, follow the path between the cottages and onto a broad track through open woodland to reach a cross path and a four-way sign on a little cairn (this point will be visited again towards the end of the walk - take note!)

Take the path to the left, to the Fairy Steps and Hazelslack.

2.   The track goes up through a plantation of tall conifers and emerges onto a limestone scarp with fine views towards the Kent estuary and Arnside Knott, especially when the trees are bare. Straight ahead are the 'Fairy Steps', a narrow cleft in the rocks of the scarp, down which you have to squeeze to continue on the path.

> An alternative route is available, (to avoid the squeeze) by going some 400m along the scarp to the right. Descend to a lower path, turn left and in a few metres, after going through a broken wall, turn left on to a faint path to reach a larger path. Turn left and follow this to reach the sign to Hazelslack below the Fairy Steps).

3.   Bearing right, follow the sign to Hazelslack, down through the woods to a second and lesser scarp through which there is another, wider cleft, with man-made steps at right angles to the path. This is part of the 'coffin' route to Beetham, for burial, in the days before there was a church at Arnside. Continue on down through Underlaid wood to reach a gate. Cross two fields, with a wall on the left, to the road near Hazelslack Tower Farm and its 14th Century pele tower.

4.   On reaching the road, leave the Limestone Link path and turn right for 250m to a stile and footpath sign on the right. Over the stile bear slightly left, off the cart track, to another stone stile in a corner of the field, and then continue by the wall on the left along two fields. Cross the far corner of the second field to a stile beside a gate and go through a narrow neck of woodland to another field.

5.   Bear half right to a wooden stile leading into the woods again. Cross the stile and follow a narrow footpath with yellow waymarks to reach a wide track at a four-way finger post. Turn right (signed Beetham Fell and Slackhead) and after about 250m, where the track curves right, leave it for a path (yellow waymark on post) going straight ahead.

Climb up through the wood, going through a gap in an old deer fence, eventually reaching some open grassland on Beetham Fell. Here you will find a small cairn with direction indicators on top.

6.   Take the path towards Beetham, on a more pronounced track. As you re-enter the wood, just before the path goes through a broken wall.
Turn left down an indistinct path through the trees, and shortly go over a stile in the wall on the right. Continue following the path steeply downhill, passing between a field for pheasant rearing on the left and a large beech tree on the right, until the cairn, mentioned earlier in the walk, is reached.

At this point turn left, signed Beetham, and almost immediately fork right, leaving a track to the left marked Private. About 100m after going through a gap in another ruined wall, and just before a left-hand bend, turn sharp left on a narrower path. This soon goes left again, round the wall of a derelict cottage garden, and comes to a stile in front of the cottage. Cross the stile and continue down through the wood and along its boundary to find another stile leading to the fields above Beetham village. Go down the field to the road and turn right to reach the Wheatsheaf Inn, the church and the start of the walk.

WALK NO. 4
Spindle Woods and Paddy Lane
8km (5 miles)   400ft of climb

This walk starts from Kendal and crosses the higher ground to the East, under Benson Knott. Spindle Wood is now only a remnant of its former self, but its beautiful mature trees do much to enhance the views across the town from that side of the valley. Paddy Lane marks the eastern boundary of Kendal for a good part of its length and gives fine views towards the Lakeland fells.

OS map 1:25,000 OL7 North Sheet.

Start
From the Town Hall in Kendal cross the top of Lowther Street and go along

Highgate and turn left down Yard 39, a cobbled ginnel running beside one of Kendal's famous snuff factories. At the bottom turn right for a few paces and enter a small private car park on the left, from where steps in the corner lead down to the riverside. Turn right, downstream, and cross the footbridge.

Turn right for a few yards and then go up Parr Street. After crossing the humped backed bridge over the former Lancaster canal, fork diagonally right up a tarmac path through Fletcher Park. Continue through a kissing gate and over the shoulder of Castle Hill by a wall on the right to reach an enclosed path through the cemetery. Follow this path to Parkside Rd.

1. Turn left along Parkside road for 200m. Just beyond the entrance to Archer's Meadow estate (opposite the cricket ground) go up a narrow footpath which starts on the right, next to an electricity substation. It zigzags alongside a wall and goes uphill behind the older houses. Go over a cross path then steeply uphill and over a stile. At the top of the hill there is a fine view of Kendal

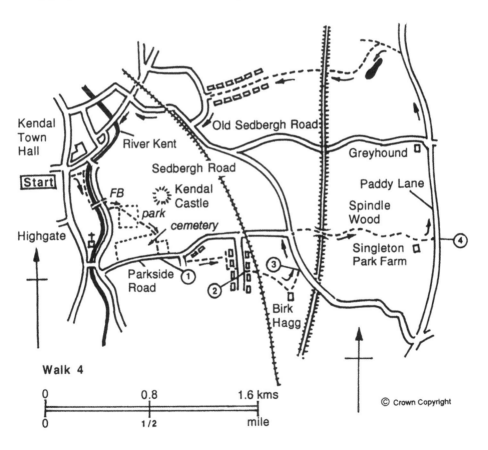

Walk 4

0   0.8   1.6 kms

0   1/2   mile

© Crown Copyright

Castle. Continue down to a stile, near houses, leading into a walled path. Turn right, then left just past the second house to reach Valley Drive.

2. Cross Valley Drive to the walled path opposite, signed Singleton Parks Road. Follow this over the Oxenholme to Windermere branch railway, passing over a beck to reach a cart track through a gate, then going half left past Birk Hagg   In 200m you reach the Sedbergh road.

3. Turn left down the road for 350m to the first junction, Look for a narrow walled path on the right, starting immediately to the right of a drive, signposted Spindle Woods and Paddy Lane. Climb this path for 100m. Cross the stile at the top and continue straight on over a railway bridge, (the main line from Euston to Scotland this time) to reach a field by another stile beside a gate.

Keep by the wall on the right to another gate with stile alongside, and then follow the beck, fording it above where two becks meet. Now head up the hill past an electricity pole, keeping by the hedge on the right, to reach another gate and stile. Bear slightly left up the next field to a gate. The cleft hill over on the left is Benson Knott. Continue straight across the next two fields via a stile left of Singleton Park Farm to emerge onto Paddy Lane by a narrow step stile.

4. Turn left along the lane for 700m to the crossroads, from where a short cut may be taken back to Kendal via the Old Sedbergh Road. Otherwise continue along Paddy Lane for about another 600m, mainly downhill, to a fingerpost on the left, signed, "Kendal via Fowl Ing Lane".

5. Follow the wall on the left down this wide track to another gate at the bottom and with a stile beside it. Enter a walled lane and after about 50m look for a narrow stile on the left. Go over this and take the path ahead descending gently through the rough heathland to a squeeze stile.

From here the path crosses the bed of the former Lower Bird's Park reservoir, close to the line of the old dam, and rises up a steep bank at the far side (the remains of the old dam.) Here turn right a short distance, between fence and wall, to another stile on the left. Follow the wall on the left down to the main line railway, crossing under it via a stile on this side, a very low tunnel, and an opening on the far side. Keep by the wall on the right to join a cart track descending to the Sandylands estate.

Go straight down the road, Peat Lane, turn left at the bottom then right at the next T-junction, to reach the town by passing under a railway bridge and eventually Stramongate Bridge over the Kent.

WALK NO. 5

Sprint and Kent Circuit

9km (5½ miles)   Undulating

The fast flowing River Kent and its tributaries, the Mint and Sprint, which join it just north of Kendal, hold many attractions for the walker at all seasons of the year. This walk includes two riverside paths, linked by a scenic high level fell road, with a few intricate field paths, muddy in places, to complete the circuit.

Drive (or go by bus) to Burneside from Kendal. Turn right at the staggered crossroads, in the centre of the village signposted Longsleddale and Skelsmergh. Park somewhere just past the entrance to Croppers Paper Mill, near Hall Park estate on the north-east side of the village.
Map Ref: SD 508958

OS map 1:25,000 OL7 North Sheet.

Start
Turn East, using the fenced path on the left beyond the estate, parallel to the road. Continue past Burneside Hall, an old fortified farmhouse. Keep right at the road junction and continue straight ahead, past the left turn, to reach Sprint Bridge.

1. Cross the bridge and take the gap on the left just beyond it, marked Dales Way, and then follow the riverbank to Sprint Mill. Go ahead through a gate in front of you, and go up the bank to continue along and above the river. Just after passing the Thirlmere aqueduct, where it crosses the river in a pipe, the path continues left over a wooden stile in a fence. Close by the riverbank, pass the converted mill buildings at Oak Bank. After another 400m you reach a footbridge over the old mill leat, at the end of a bank of trees on the right.

Cross the bridge and then a stile, and across the field to a small gate, leaving the riverbank for a while, and across a farm drive, through another small gate and bear left, ascending with a hedge on your right to join a cart track going through a gate and over the hill. Aim just right of the trees across the next field to rejoin the riverbank, high above the water at this point.

Follow the track, descending through trees, and look for a wooden stile and slab bridge on the left at the bottom of the bank, leading across a field to a road close to Gurnal Bridge. Cross the bridge and continue up the road, for 150m, to find a stone step stile on the right. Go diagonally up the field to another stile to the left of the barn. Cross the farm drive to go through a field gate opposite, then immediately through the field gate on the left.

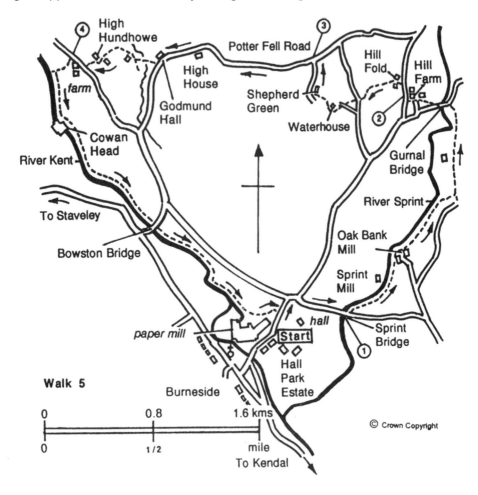

Walk 5

Turn right up the field to a ladder stile. Ahead, with a hedge on the right, cross the stile (and the drive to the Old Stone Barn) to reach the road.

2.   Turn right along the road for about 150m, passing Hill Farm on the right to reach to Hill Fold Farm on the left. Turn up the drive past the house. Go between the house and the stock sheds. Cross the stile and bear left across the field to the opposite corner. Climb the stile in the wall close to where it joins a fence.

Ahead, with a wall on the left enter a green lane. At the junction turn right for a few metres to a gate on the left. Then head up the field to a metal ladder stile. Cross the drive and go through the wooden gate opposite.

Continue to another drive and bear right to go through a small gate. Turn right, round the outside of the garden of the house, to another gate. After the gate aim half right, walking round a planted area to a plank bridge and a gate over a small beck. Aim for the buildings of Shepherd Green, going through a gate and then going to the left of most of the buildings to reach the drive. Turn right for 200m to reach Potter Fell road.

3.   Turn left along the fell road with views of Kendal to the left and, on a clear day, the Coniston fells ahead,. Follow the road for about 1.5km until it drops down past High House Farm on the left, then the dormer-windowed Godmund Hall on the right. Just beyond the Hall leave the road to follow the footpath sign on the right across the field to a stile.

Cross a narrow drive to a track which leads to another stone stile and go down a small path by the beck to a footbridge. Cross and continue up the field towards a stile and some buildings.

Turn right along the drive, going through a waymarked gate on the same line beyond the house. Follow the bridleway with the beck below on the right. At a three-way junction, near a large sycamore tree, follow the bridleway sign left to Hundhowe through a gate. Pass the fine old barn with its stone water trough on the left and go down the drive to the road.

4.   Turn right along the road for 150m, and just past the buildings of Hag Foot, follow the footpath sign on the left, going through the farmyard and down a rough track leading to the River Kent.

Do not cross the bridge but go through the kissing gate on the left to follow the river bank. It is now about 2.5km back to Burneside.

You soon pass the vast new housing development at Cowan Head Mill. Go past Bowston Bridge and continue along the riverbank to Burneside When the paper mill is reached follow the path round the edge of its large buildings to reach the road at the start of the walk.

WALK No. 6

Patton and Docker
9.6km (6miles)   Undulating

This is an undulating walk through fields, with some quiet road walking. The route follows the Dales Way Long Distance footpath for about 2 miles. The paths are well waymarked almost throughout. On a clear day there are fine views of the surrounding fells.

The walk starts in Meal Bank north east of Kendal. Take the A6. out of Kendal. In about 1.6 miles turn right, signposted Meal Bank. After about a mile of winding road turn right, signposted Meal Bank Mill Trading Estate with Meal Bank hamlet beyond. There is a small (not public) parking area here. Map Reference SD 541956.

OS map 1:25,000 OL 7   North Sheet.

Start
Walk back over the river up to the Patton road. Turn left for 20m then follow the Footpath sign for Garnett Folds on the right, up a shallow valley, which is littered with Shap granite 'erratic' boulders brought down by the last ice sheet. Climb a stile over a wire fence and continue up the hill keeping just right of a small beck, to reach a corner where a wall meets a fence. Follow the fence / hedge, then a wall on the left to the next stile, just beyond a gnarled ash tree. Bear slightly right, and immediately after passing the ruins of Littlemire Farm turn sharp right uphill, to a gateway at the top of the field. Beyond this, follow an old sunken track between ruined walls over the hill to reach a gate onto a narrow lane.

1. Turn left up the lane for 30m, then go over a stile on your right next to a locked gate. Go through the next gate and then diagonally left up the field to another gate in the top left hand corner. Here you can see a fenced off old quarry to the left of the path, which continues alongside a wall on the right. Cross a wooden stile in a stopped-up gateway on the right, just before another gate. Now keep by the wall on the left for approximately 50m, then bear right, aiming towards the buildings ahead, passing a fenced-off small tarn on your left.

Climb a ladder stile in the corner of the wall. Follow the wall on the left to a second ladder stile, cross this and then bear right aiming for a stile in the corner at New House. Here you join the Dales Way. In front of the house turn right, up the hill beside the pylon. From the top of the hill there are fine views of Whinfell ridge with the Howgills further to the right. These are about 400m years old from the Silurian age. Immediately in front is Black Moss Tarn, a home for water birds.

2. Descend to the left of the tarn, crossing a wooden footbridge to a stile in a wall. Turn left to follow a wall / fence on the left to a stone step stile ahead. Then follow a hedge on the right to a stile in the corner. Use the stepping stones to cross the wet ground. Follow a wall on the left to reach Biglands via a stile and gate. Pass in front of the house and follow the drive to reach Patton road.

3. Cross the road and follow a rather overgrown track opposite, that goes through a gate to pass High Barn on your left, then another gate, partially hidden by trees to pass Low Barn on the right. Turn right along a track to a field gate. About 50m past the gate bear left to pass through an old metal kissing gate onto the drive to the large complex of Shaw End. Turn right along the drive for about 400m to a metal gate and kissing gate on the left. Go down the field to the footbridge over the River Mint. Cross the bridge and bear right uphill and across the field to a field gate (20m to the right of a ruined barn). Pass through this gate to a track ahead to a hedge corner. At this point the West Coast Main Line comes into view. Continue with the hedge on the right. Cross the two waymarked stiles, while dropping down to the bridge over Thursgill Beck. Climb the steep road ahead to emerge onto A685 Grayrigg Road.

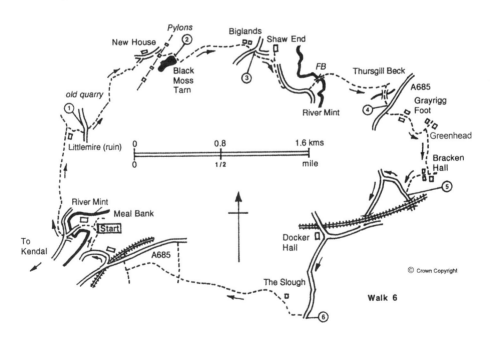

4. Turn right along the A685 for 80m then turn left up the drive to Grayrigg Foot Farm. Pass through between the buildings, through a gate ahead and over the footbridge and through the gate, keeping by a hedged stream on the right. After 90m, curve left to reach the drive to Greenhead. Before reaching a bungalow, turn right (waymarked) to a gate near the corner of the field, leaving the Dales Way at this point. Keep straight ahead over the hill, 20m to the right of a large oak tree, to reach a gate into the next field.

Then bear right, aiming for a solitary large sycamore tree and Bracken Hall beyond. Climb a stile leading between the buildings, and then turn right, just beyond the house. The farm drive is not a Public Right of Way. After the cattle grid bear left, with a hedge on your left. Dip down and then up to a stile close to the railway, joining a road.

5. Turn right, and at the next minor road turn sharply left, following Flodder Beck, to pass under the impressive six arched limestone mainline railway viaduct (1846). In 100m, turn right at the T junction for 300m, as far as the next junction (ignoring a drive on the left to Tenter End). Turn left onto Docker Lane, for 600m. Pass under the supergrid power line and in about 120m turn right, through a gate (signed Meal Bank).

6. Turn left down the field to cross a grassed bridge over the beck. Turn right to a wooden kissing gate in a wall ahead. Cross into the next field keeping above the beck, to reach a gate into the paddock at The Slough. Climb diagonally left to a ladder stile. Turn right, then keep straight on towards a facing wall. Turn left along the wall to a stile with a stream and footbridge beyond. Cross the beck and go straight up the steep bank through the trees and across the field, to the right of some small old quarries, to cross a wooden step stile into the next field. Keep going ahead, at first slightly up, then downhill, aiming between two large trees, to reach a gate. Follow the track slightly downhill, passing about 20m to the right of a waterworks building, and then crossing a ruined wall and a small stream. Go through sparse woodland to find a stone gap stile in the next wall, just right of a larch tree. Benson Knott is up on your left. Dip down over the beck and then keep on in the same direction for 300m, following the contours then slightly downhill, and look for a high step stile in the next cross wall. This is difficult to see until you get closer to the wall. Now keep along the contours to enter a stony walled track just below a stone barn, and from here descend to the A685.

Opposite is the former tollhouse on the Kendal to Appleby turnpike. Turn left along the road for 200m. Just after crossing a railway bridge, turn sharp right down into Meal Bank. At the start of a wood turn right down an unmade lane back into the industrial estate and the start of the walk.

WALK No. 7

Underbarrow and Lord's Lot
9.6km (6miles)   500ft of climb

This walk is entirely within the Lake District National Park and visits the scattered villages of Underbarrow and Crosthwaite, and some rough upland pastures, including Lord's Lot, from where fine views can be obtained. The walk is unsuitable in misty conditions, as distant landmarks are necessary for navigation.

Take the Underbarrow Road due west of Kendal for about 3 miles. Turn right in the village of Underbarrow and park near the Church. Map Ref: SD 464926

OS map OL7 1:25,000   North Sheet.

Start
With the church behind you walk a few metres back to the road. Turn right, down the road past the old school. Just beyond the bridge, descend a stile on the left keeping straight ahead to a small wicketgate into a field. Turn right and follow the hedge along to a wall stile where the hedge ends. Over the stile follow the hedge on the left to another stile, then aim towards the buildings ahead (The Broom), to cross a high ladder stile. Continue to a gate, then turn right, through the drive of the house and out onto a metalled road.

1. Go straight across the road and up a rough track opposite, to a stile and gate. Keep by the wall on the left for about 400m, until a stile and gate give access to a walled track. Turn right and go downhill, for about 70m to a wooden stile on the left at the corner of a wood. Go up the steep bank, following waymarks and bear right heading for a large oak tree.

At the top of the hill there are fine views, both behind, of the Lyth valley, the Kent estuary and Arnside Knott, and ahead, northwards to the Kentmere Fells. The view ahead includes two farms, aim for the left-hand one, Low Fold, following the line of the walls on the left

Turn right before reaching the farm gate and follow the track uphill until you reach a conspicuous ladder stile. Climb the stile and keep by the wall on the right to another stile and then onto a cart track leading to a crossways about 100m short of Low Fold.

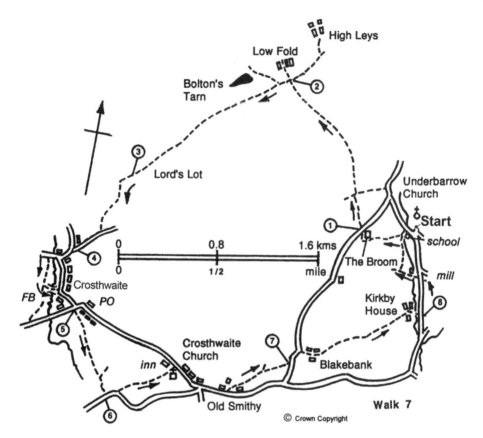

2. Turn left, and shortly bear half left, leaving the track for another ladder stile that leads to open pasture again. Keep straight ahead between the hills.

The hill on the right conceals Bolton's Tarn, now overgrown but still a fine habitat for wetland species. When you reach a cross wall climb a wooden stile (not the gateway) into Lord's Lot itself. Turn left by the wall. At the top turn right to a small top. The summit cairn may then be seen in the distance. After reaching the top, find a path down through the gorse, heading N W towards the Langdale Pikes (if visible) or to a small gate by a holly bush. At this wall / fence turn left and soon find a stony path down.

In about 500m, when you emerge from the gorse, look for a wooden stile next to a field gate where a wall meets a fence. Beck nearby.

3. Cross the stile and head for a waymark post 50m ahead. Continue downhill on the track for 120m, curving left for 50m to a second waymark post.

22

Go down the track as far as the gate and turn right to follow the hedge on the left. At the end of the hedge look for a metal gate leading into a walled lane. Follow this lane right, to the road.

4. Turn left along the road and right at the T-junction, signposted to Hubbersty Head. Cross the bridge and then climb the stile on the left just beyond it. Follow the fence on the right over the hill and down to another stile. Now bear left over wet ground, to a wooden kissing gate leading to an interesting old clapper bridge, and so to the road again. Turn right for about 240m to Crosthwaite, and a major road.

5. Cross the major road and follow the footpath sign between the houses opposite, down a bank to a wicketgate. Cross the field to the stile opposite, and keep going in the same direction through various stiles and wall gaps, first with the wall on the right, then on the left, and then on the right again. Eventually you descend to a gate in the corner of the last field, giving access to a farm road. Follow this unmetalled road right for about 200m to a metalled road.

6. Turn left up the road for 50m and then go left up a bridleway (very muddy when wet) that crosses the shoulder of Church Bank and leads directly to Crosthwaite Church. Go straight through the churchyard, passing the church door, and out through a stile and up a path behind the Punch Bowl Inn to the main road. Turn right along the road towards Kendal for about 500m. At the old smithy take a road to the left amongst cottages. Beyond the cottages the road becomes a cart track for some 30m before it takes a left-hand bend, go through a low stone stile on the right. Go diagonally over the shoulder of the hill to reach a gate onto a metalled by-road.

7. Turn left and after about 100m go right, down the drive to Blakebank. The Right of Way passes immediately in front of the house and down a broad grassy path to a gate at the bottom of the garden. It is now about 1000m to Kirkby House. Continue beside the wall / hedge on the left, keeping to the top of a spur, until you drop down into a walled track and reach a bridge over a small beck.

Bear left to a stile, and then follow the wall on the right to another stile, from where you follow the bottom of a bank towards the modern barn ahead. Enter the farmyard of Kirkby House by a stile and a gate at the left-hand end of the barn, and go between the buildings and out along the drive, over Chapel Beck, to the road.

8. Turn left along the road for 300m and then turn left down a yard (with large trucks) to the old water mill buildings, sadly now showing few signs of their

former use. Go behind the former mill buildings and up a track to a gate. Ahead is a really fine specimen of an oak tree, growing from an outcrop. Go up the bank and round the far side of the tree to see it to best advantage then drop down to the beck. Shortly you will see a waymark post and a small clapper bridge crossing this beck, which presumably served as a leat for the water mill. Cross here and continue along by the beck to reach the small gate used just after starting the walk.

WALK No 8
WINSTER VALLEY 1
10.4km (6.5 miles)   Undulating

Drive west from Kendal on the Crook Road, B5284 for about 7miles. Go past the Windermere Golf Club. Park in a lay-by on the right hand side of the road just before the 30 mph sign, about ½ mile beyond the entrance to Windermere Golf Club. Walk down the road for about 100m to reach the drive to the Linthwaite House Hotel on the left.   SD 406957

OS map OL7 1:25,000 North Sheet

Start
Follow the narrow signposted path (could be overgrown in Summer) to the left of the hotel drive until it meets the drive again.   Turn left and continue on an enclosed path alongside the drive beside ornamental duck ponds. On reaching a wooden kissing gate go up the field, towards a clump of trees at the top of the hill where there is a telegraph pole (not an electricity pole which is to the right of this). Go down to the right-hand of two gates seen ahead and follow the telephone line across the field to the gate near the house.

Go through the gate and then past the end of the house, down a rough path to a steep stile in a wall, leading to the drive of Lindeth Farm.

1. Turn right along the drive and go through the farmyard to a gate which has a sign 'TO THE KENNELS'.

There is a waymark on a post several metres beyond the gate. Follow a good track across two fields to reach a walled drive to a house. Pass the house on your right and follow the waymark on the electricity pole beyond, to reach a gate into a rough pasture. (This is where the return route meets the outward route).

Just past the gate go down some rough steps next to the wall on the right and continue by the wall to an iron kissing gate. Through the gate, follow the path and cross a drive to reach a wooden kissing gate.

Then bear left along a rough green track as it snakes between many stone outcrops and eventually reaches the Bowness to Levens Bridge road (A5074).

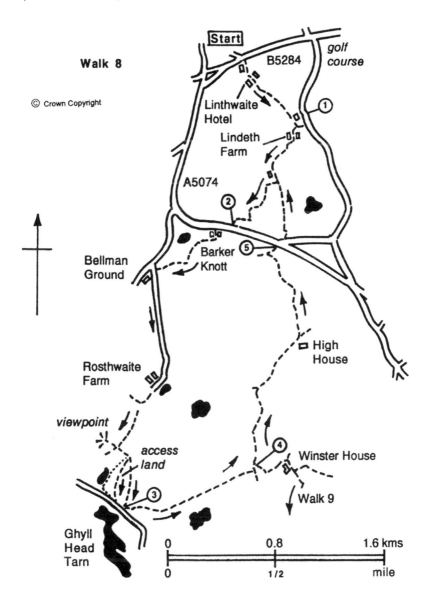

2. Turn right along the road for about 100 metres. On the left enter Barker Knott with its interesting old buildings. Go through the farmyard and out on a stony track via an iron gate signposted 'Bellman Houses'.

When this track bears left uphill, leave it and follow the wall on the right with a large tarn to be seen over the wall. Keep by the wall/hedge/wall (passing through a gate on the way) almost to the set of converted farm buildings at Bellman Ground. Go over a wooden stile and turn left up a metalled drive. Follow this drive for about 700m as far as Rosthwaite Farm.

Go through the left hand of two formidable modern gateways and follow the drive round to the left of all the buildings. Continue past a large pond to reach a gate with a stone stile on the left, leading to a track across the open fell. Follow this undulating track for about 500m, to where, near the top of a hill, a signpost indicates a Public Footpath to the left. (A short detour to the right leads to an excellent viewpoint with a stone seat looking over Windermere and to the fells beyond). Follow the Public Footpath to a kissing gate. Go through this and continue on through a tall gate in a deer fence then through another kissing gate on the immediate right.

This leads through the Ghyll Head Access Area, an attractive piece of land owned by the National Park Authority, to emerge on to the Ghyll Head road. Across the road is Ghyll Head Tarn, used for fishing.

3. Turn left through the adjacent kissing gate following the path, signposted Winster House, which bears right in front of the next kissing gate and continues across rough open pasture. Continue ahead through a gate in a fence, eventually to reach a stony track going along beside a wall.

4. Turn left along this stony track and follow it for about 1 km, as it gradually descends towards High House, keeping right and ignoring all tracks to the left. Where the track turns right, do not go through the gate marked 'PRIVATE' or through the field gate straight ahead, but bear left alongside a wall to go through two gates. Continue alongside the wall on the right for about 600m, eventually to reach a grassy lane going right to meet the A5074 road again.

5. Cross the road and go up the track opposite for several metres until reaching a signposted stone stile in the wall on the left. Go over this, then under the power lines and round to the left of the rocky hill in front. Continue following the power lines and go through a gate which leads via more rough pasture to the junction with the outward route at another gate. Go through this gate and follow the outward route, via Lindeth Farm, back to the start.

WALK NO. 9

Winster Valley 2
11.2km (7 miles)   Undulating

The remarks in the introduction to Walk No 8 about the Winster valley also apply to this walk. It is however advisable to follow this walk after the grass is cut, because of possible damage to the crop and also for your own comfort, particularly in wet weather. The whole walk is very muddy after rain.

Take the Underbarrow and Crosthwaite road to Bowland Bridge about 7 miles West of Kendal. There is parking space near the telephone kiosk.
Map Ref: SD 418896.

OS map OL7 1:25,000 North Sheet.

Start
Take the road signposted to Witherslack and Grange, beside the Hare and Hounds and after 100m cross a stile on the left near an electricity pole. Keep by the wall on the right across the first two fields, then cross a corner stile and stay by the wall, which is now on your left. After another stile you reach open pasture; keep straight ahead, left of the power line, to pass left of a barn, and continue to a stile onto a byroad. On this stretch two waymarks are helpful.

1.   Cross the road slightly left, to a signposted path through large metal gates. Cross the field to join a cart track. After going through the gate into the third field, bear half left to a stile in the left-hand wall. Go over the stile and straight across the field to a gate opposite, beyond a small beck.

Bear right through the gateway and follow the left-hand side of the wall/hedge past a waymark then over the top of the hill, through two stiles and down to a gate at the bottom of the third field. From the gate bear right to follow the wall to a stile onto a minor road. Cross the road by the two stiles, following the wall on the left to a third stile. Now keep straight ahead reaching the A5074 at another stile by the gate.

2.   Turn right along the road to another signposted stile on the left, then keep left to a gate into a small paddock. Cross this to another gate into a broad track. Turn right to pass in front of the cottages then go through a waymarked field gate on the left at the end of the buildings. Follow the wall down to another gate, then cross this field to another waymarked field gate. Now follow the hedge on the left to a stile in the far corner of the field, go through and turn

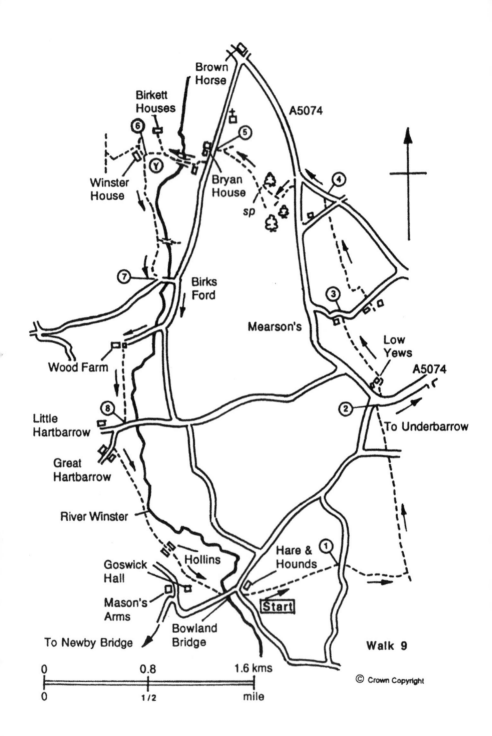

Brown
Horse

Birkett
Houses

A5074

⑥

⑤

Y

Winster
House

Bryan
House

sp

④

③

⑦

Birks
Ford

Mearson's

Low
Yews

A5074

Wood Farm

⑧

Little
Hartbarrow

②

To Underbarrow

Great
Hartbarrow

River Winster

Hollins

Hare &
Hounds

①

Goswick
Hall

Mason's
Arms

Start

To Newby Bridge

Bowland
Bridge

Walk 9

© Crown Copyright

0   0.8   1.6 kms

0   1/2   mile

right to follow the hedge which is now on your right. After crossing the next stile, keep by the hedge on the right to another stile, then follow the hedge uphill and across the field to reach a drive to a nearby house. Cross the drive and the mown grass to another wall stile onto a minor road.

3. Turn right up the road and after about 300m turn left at a footpath sign and go up a stony track through a small wood, to cross a small bridge to a gate in the corner, leading into a field. Keep by the left-hand boundary, crossing one stone stile and two ladder stiles, after which go down by the wall on the right, past a spring, to a gate in the wall leading to two wooden stiles crossing a drive. Now keep straight ahead by the plantation on the right to reach a stile onto another road in the far corner of the field.

4. Turn left along the by-road to reach the A5074 again. Then turn left onto the main road for about 100m to the signposted footpath on the right in a lay-by. Over the stile bear left, through a new gate in the fence towards the wood, crossing a small beck and boggy ground to reach a gate in the bottom corner.

Now bear half right, to go up the steep slope between the trees.
A waymark near the top points left as the old track zigzags up the slope. You soon come to a three-way signpost, where you turn sharp right again to go between two free-standing gateposts onto a stony track. Follow this track as it curves round below the trees on the left, continuing for a further 500m to reach a road at Bryan House Farm. Winster Church lies to the north.

5. Turn left along the road past Bryan House Farm and in about 100m turn right down the signposted drive to Winster House. After a bridge as you pass a recently created lake on the left, ignore the drive to Birkett House, and keep on straight ahead.

Then, as you round a right-hand bend near some rhododendrons, at a waymark go through a gap on the left, over a stile, onto a grassy track going sharp back to the left below Winster House.

6. Follow the grassy track and keep a hedge, then a wall on your left before reaching open fields above the River Winster. Keep by the river across the next fields over a stile, with a waymarked post directly ahead, to join a track coming down from the right near an old kiln, (This was once used for burning green bracken to make potash, used in the production of lye for washing fleeces). Continuing in the same direction, follow this track along the field, ignoring a footbridge on the left, to reach a minor road via a track through the wood on the right. Turn left down the minor road to reach Birks Ford and its old stone clapper bridge.

7. Cross the bridge and turn right along the road for 300m, then turn right into the drive to Wood Farm. On reaching the buildings before the house go round the left hand end of the barn and follow a green lane with an old orchard on the right. Leave the lane at the waymarked gate, part way along on the left, and cross two fields. Bear slightly right, uphill, to a gate in the far upper corner of the second field, near a wood. Continue along the contours to reach another byroad by a track that runs between walls beside a small wood.

8. Turn right up the road for about 200m and, just before Great Hartbarrow Farm, take the signposted track on the left to Hollins farm. It is now about 1.3km back to Bowland Bridge. Cross two short fields and go through the left hand of two gateways at the end of the second field, just beyond a small clapper bridge. Cross the next field to a gate at the far side. Now follow the wall on the left and go into a walled lane leading to Hollins Farm.

Go through the gate and pass immediately in front of the house, (past an old cheese press on the right). Keep on up the drive, and just beyond the end of the garden go through a small gate on the left, leading via a permissive path into the next field. Turn right in the field and keep by the wall to a gate. Cross to a stile near the middle of the next hedge to reach a field near Goswick Hall. Now aim for a waymark near a hawthorn tree, and then keep by the wall on the right to reach a waymarked gap in the corner of a wood.

Continue to a kissing gate in a wire fence and on through the wood to emerge into a field near a large oak tree. Cross the field diagonally left to reach a kissing gate onto the road near Bowland Bridge and the starting point.

WALK NO 10

Under Whinfell

11.2km (7miles) Undulating

This unspoilt part of Kendal's local countryside is dominated at every point by views of Whinfell Beacon to the N E.

The start is just before Grayrigg on the A685 Kendal to Tebay road. One mile after crossing the mainline railway, there is a small lay-by between the entrance to `Kapellan' (the animal shelter set up by A. W. Wainwright and his second wife) and the drive to Ghyll Bank, marked by fingerpost. Park here. Map Ref: SD 571970.

OS map OL7   1:25,000   North Sheet.

Start

Walk up the road towards Tebay and, after a few metres, turn left and follow the right-hand drive past Ghyll Bank and through a gate at the end of the yard, to descend into a delightful secluded valley. Follow the track through a gate, past the converted buildings of Bye Mill, with the old mill leat up on your right. 250m beyond the buildings cross a footbridge over the beck. Continue alongside the minor stream on the left, with a line of trees coming in from the right after 100m, until a gate is reached. Continue through the gate and up a rise ahead to reach another gate with a road beyond.

1. Turn left along the road for about 600m, with fine views of Whinfell Beacon over on the right. Pass the drives of Low and High Deepslack farms to reach a crossroads.

2. Turn left here and after 350m take a field gate on the right by an ash tree. Bear half right past a telegraph pole and an isolated tree. At this point turn right down into a small valley aiming for the outer corner of a wall / fence.

Keeping the fence on your left climb about 50m to find a stile. Turn left here and follow the contours to reach Stone Hall, an old farm.

Pass through three gates and then out onto the farm drive. In 100m turn left onto a road. Walk 400m along this road as far Chapel House, a former Methodist chapel, and the Old School House.   Walk another 150m down the road, turn back right at the junction and then in another 150m take a finger post sign, left, towards Whinfell Tarn.

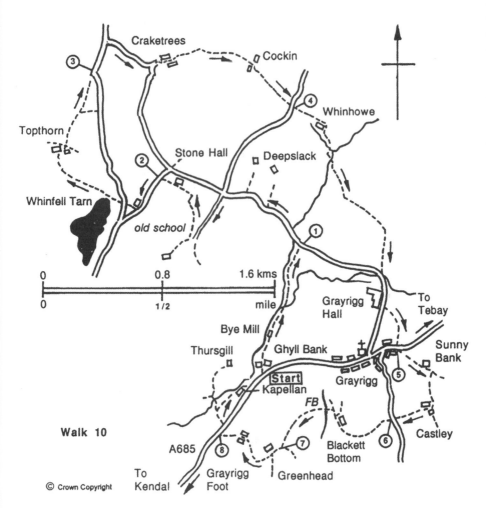

Bear half right away from the tarn. In 250m look for a wooden stile in the middle of the far fence. Continue in the same direction to a gate into a farm drive. Turn right along the drive to reach Topthorn, a large farm with converted buildings. Take the right hand fork and then the centre of three drives. Pass in front of the house to the right and leave by waymarked step stile and soon a small waymarked gate into a green lane. At the end of the lane go through a gate into a field, then continue towards a gateway at the end of the field, with Whinfell Beacon directly in ahead.

Keep along the lower part of the next field with a wire fence on the left. Climb a step stile at the far end, then go up half right to a stile indicated by a finger post by a wall corner leading into a lane.

32

3. Go left up the lane as far as the next junction. Turn right for 450m to reach the entrance to Craketrees, (signed Whinfell Nurseries on a plaque in the wall) at a corner. Continue straight ahead past the house and weave through some sheds to find a double gate into a field. Aim to the right of the barn across the field and go through a gate in the far corner near a large sycamore tree. Climb up the next field aiming to the left hand end of a short section of fence ahead. Cross straight over a drive, and up and over a rise, to find a gate at the left hand end of the next wall. Continue by the wall on the left via an open green lane to reach Cockin Farm. Pass between the farmhouse and the barn, then turn right through a gate behind the barn. Pass through a second gate then turn left up a steep rise along a wire fence to another gate 200m ahead.

Go down the following field to a step stile into a small wood next to a drinking trough, and straight through the wood to a metalled road that leads (left) up to the repeater station on Whinfell ridge.

4. Cross straight over the unfenced road and through the field to a wall stile in the far right corner. (A very awkward stile) Cross another field to a gate, before descending to a large barn at Whinhowe. Go round the far end of the barn and out onto a farm track via an opening.

After crossing over a small beck under the track, head off left, down to a footbridge over Whinhowe Gill. This happens to be the same beck you followed near the start of the walk. Cross this beck and turn right. Stay by the fence at first, then head diagonally across the field and over a wall stile marked by a wooden post opposite. Keep to the right of the old quarry, and then head half left to a gate in a fence that eventually can be seen on the hill. From here a cart track soon becomes a concrete drive leading to Grayrigg Hall Farm, seen ahead, with Grayrigg Church behind.

On reaching the farm go through a small wooden gate opposite the farmhouse. Head diagonally across the field and round the left of the hill ahead, curving round to the right go up to the main road (A685), joining it at a step stile (or gate) a few metres left of the old terraced cottages.

5. Cross the main road and go left for a short way to a footpath sign on the right, leading up a narrow path beside some gardens. Continue to follow this waymarked path to Sunny Bank, the next farm.

Pass through the farmyard and after the buildings, go through a gate and bear right off the main track and down a field, aiming for Castley Bank Farm seen ahead. Enter the farmyard by a gate and then out through another gate past the farmhouse, dated 1738, onto a drive. Follow the drive to the lane.

6. Cross the lane and go through a gate into a field. Go down the field to a small beck that leads to a waymarked gate (not the first gate on the right) at the bottom. Continue by the beck on an old cart track to Blackett Bottom. Go through three gates, passing the first group of houses and along the drive to another gate. Immediately after, head left, down the bank, and over the beck by a footbridge.

Go straight ahead, climbing over the shoulder of the hill to a field gate, then veer left along the contours across the next field and through the upper gate. Turn left by the hedge, veering right towards the end of the field to go through a double gateway. Turn right and go between two houses, part of Greenhead Farm.

7. Continue down the tarmac road for about 100m and, before reaching a cattle grid at the bottom, look for a Dales Way footpath sign on the right. Go through the gate and follow an old terraced track that leads to a gate near a footbridge over a beck. Cross the bridge and go through Grayrigg Foot Farm and out on its drive to the main road again.

The quickest way back to your car is to turn right and walk along the road for about 500m. But to avoid the traffic, in 50m turn left up the drive to Thursgill then descend to the corner of a wood. Here you leave the Dalesway and follow a narrow path, climbing obliquely up, through a splendid bluebell wood in spring. Go through a small gate onto an enclosed path behind the animal shelter at `Kapellan'.

You may not see any animals but you will certainly hear them heralding your approach. Go through another small gate. Take the steps leading down behind the garage, above a steep drop, to emerge through an opening into the visitor's car park. (Visits are by appointment only.) Turn left at the road, and walk about 100m to the starting point.

WALK No. 11

Drumlin Country
12km (7.5miles)   500ft of climb

The undulating nature of the country through which this walk passes is the result of the many drumlins, rounded hummocks of boulder clay which were carried down from the north and shaped by ice during the last ice age over 10,000 years ago. The ridges of the drumlins provide some good distant views, while the former Lancaster to Kendal canal, open to navigation from 1819 to 1955, lends interest to the area.

The walk is perhaps best avoided in the height of summer as there are many fields with long grass (for silage) and some paths are liable to be overgrown with nettles; however, there are no muddy farmyards on the route.

There is space for parking by the roadside at Leasgill a side road off the A6 between Levens Bridge and Milnthorpe, but the road will be crowded with cars at school opening and closing times. The Kendal to Milnthorpe bus stops by the village Hall. Map Reference: SD 496840

OS map OL7 1:25,000 North Sheet

Start
Keeping the Village Hall / Athanaeum Club on your left, walk north up hill for about 100m, then take the flight of concrete steps to the right which leads to a side road. Follow the side road uphill for about 400m to find a stone gap stile on the left. Go through the avenue of sycamore trees. At the end, turn left onto a bridleway for 70m before turning right at a signpost indicating Hincaster and Levens Bridge. Traverse along the slope with a wood, and later a wall, on the right, to reach High Barns Farm. Immediately before the farmhouse climb a high stone step stile and keep by the hedge on the left to reach a cart track near the cowshed.

Continue in the same direction, following the track over the hill to reach Hincaster Hall. This fine building dates from the 16th Century and is a good example of a local traditional farmhouse with its mullioned windows and round chimneys. Continue down the metalled farm drive to the road.

1.   The route continues up the bridleway signposted Wells Bridge and Lancaster Canal, opposite. A short detour as far as the end of the houses on the left is worthwhile to inspect the entrance to the canal tunnel. The tunnel

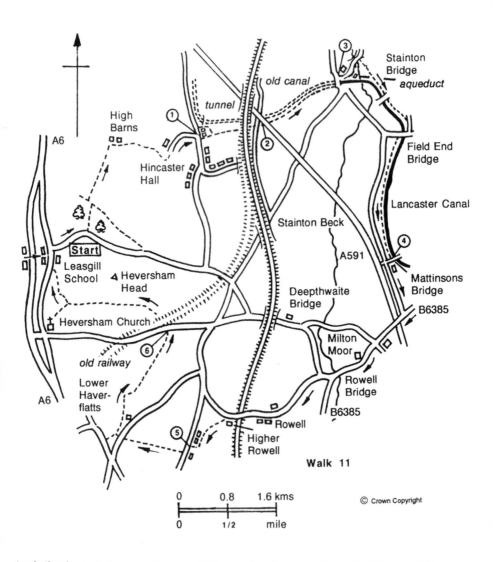

took the Lancaster canal some 350m under the drumlin called Tunnel Hill, while the barge horses were led over the top, along the bridleway. Bargees had to 'walk' their boats through the tunnel by lying on the backs and pushing along the canal walls.

To regain the route take the horse path to the right of the tunnel entrance and behind the cottages, to join the bridleway as it goes left between hedges and over the top of the hill. The bridleway and tunnel have been declared an ancient monument. Follow the path under the mainline railway and down to the road.

2.   Turn left, and then right after passing under the A591 to rejoin the sunken remains of the canal. Follow the towpath as far bridge 172, where the canal still retains water. Climb the stile under the bridge. There is no tow-path on the left of the canal for a short distance, so a short loop is needed to regain it further on.

3.   Cross the head of the canal, and go over the parking area into the lane and into the hamlet of Stainton Bridge. Continue for about 200m to the bridge over Stainton Beck.

> (A detour between the cottages on the right, at a finger post marked 'Stainton Aqueduct' will enable you to see where Stainton Beck goes under the canal. Look for a narrow path on the right, waymarked, to the left of a blue garage).

Return to the road and turn right for 100m. Just beyond the bridge cross over a stile on the right. Follow the fence on the right until you reach another stile which provides access to the tow-path on the canal embankment. Continue along the bank, to the next bridge where you climb a flight of steps to a squeeze stile and over a wooden stile to reach the canal path again. In a further 210m join Commonmire Lane by going down a steep path on the left through the trees, 150m before Field End Bridge, (No 169).

Follow the lane to the bridge where you cross over the canal to join the western bank via a slope on the left. Continue south along the towpath for about 1km to reach Mattinson's Bridge (No 168) where a right turn up some steps then down a grassy track leads past a cottage to the road. (Note that this track is not a Right of Way, but the occupier has allowed permissive access).

4. Turn left along this minor road. At the junction turn right on the B6385. Cross over the trunk road where a glance back will reveal an imposing row of drumlins. Continue along the B road for another 700m, past Milton Moor to Rowell Bridge then bear right (signposted Rowell), up a minor road, keeping straight ahead at the next junction.

After about 1km on this minor road, beyond the railway and just past Higher Rowell Farm (kennels), follow a signpost on the left through a gate and then immediately left through a second gate.

Keep by the hedge on the right, then across the middle of the next field, keeping the bungalows on the right, cross over a stile into a hedged path (possibly overgrown in summertime) leading to the road.

5. Turn left for 100m to the footpath sign on the right opposite Cragg Yeat. Go straight across the field, take the right-hand gate, continue uphill over a wooden stile to a narrow slate stile on the crest of this drumlin. Descend to another stile and across a narrow lane to a further stile. Now aim for the field gate about two thirds of the way down the field, go right, and then contour along the field, keeping the converted buildings (Lower Haverflatts) on your right, to reach a squeeze stile and a gate at the far right-hand corner. Keep by the hedge along the next field, and then go over a waymarked ladder stile on the right. Follow the left hand hedge for 40m and then turn left through a squeeze stile.

Follow the right hand edge of the field to a stile in the far right corner. From here the route descends, to the right of a lone tree to a stile opposite the right-hand end of the tree belt ahead.

6. Turn left along the road and almost immediately turn right through a gateway, to cross the dismantled Arnside to Hincaster railway and reach the playing fields of Dallam School. Bear slightly left to a stile in the curved wall across the playing field, and then go diagonally up the slope, aiming right of a clump of trees.

Keep above these trees to pass below a second clump, (waymarked) then contour round the hill, with fine views of the Kent estuary, descending towards the left side of the wood ahead. From here a kissing gate gives access to a track through the wood. Turn right on to a lane which leads down hill to Leasgill, and the start of the walk.

Drumlins. These are glacial deposits, smoothed into oval shaped hills by a flowing ice sheet. Seen here against the backdrop of the Howgills. See paragraph 4 in the text.

WALK NO. 12

Birkbeck Fells and Bretherdale
15 km (8 miles)   800ft of climb

This walk starts about 10 miles north of Kendal on the A6. It crosses Birkbeck Fells, a moorland area of grass and heather with wide views to the east, then descends to the hamlet of Greenholme. The return route visits the remote valley of Bretherdale. Do choose a clear day. Parts of this walk are very wet underfoot.

Travel north up the A6 from Kendal and leave the car, or the Shap bus, at the car park on the right marked by a memorial stone just before you reach the summit of the hill after climbing from Huck's Bridge. There is a stile and gate in the fence on the right shortly before the car park which is where the walk finishes. Map Ref: NY 554062.

OS map OL7 1:25,000 North Sheet

Start
Walk north up the road for about 600m passing a TV repeater station on the left and going under a set of power lines, then climb a stile on the right, beside a gate, and follow a good gravel track for a further 1 km. As you approach the forestry plantation and about 100 metres before reaching the gate, go through a waymarked gate on the right onto a hard track and follow this across the moor. Ignore the left fork leading to a shooting hut, keep to the main track until its end just past the highest point and near a white gas marker post set in concrete.

Just beyond the barn, near a low boulder, leave the line of the main track and go half right down the slope, aiming just left of the mature pine trees in the valley bottom. Soon you will find another faint track.

1. A rougher track now commences, going left past the summit of Crag Hill (with a cairn). A detour to the cairn will give a good view of the route ahead towards Tebay, and the ruined barn that is the next objective.

Follow the faint sunken old bridleway to the south west, (ignoring any modern vehicle tracks) as it snakes round and eventually reaches the ruined barn at Nan Hill that goes above the ruined farmhouse at Eskew Head. With the stream on your right, go left through a gateway in the wall, leading to a

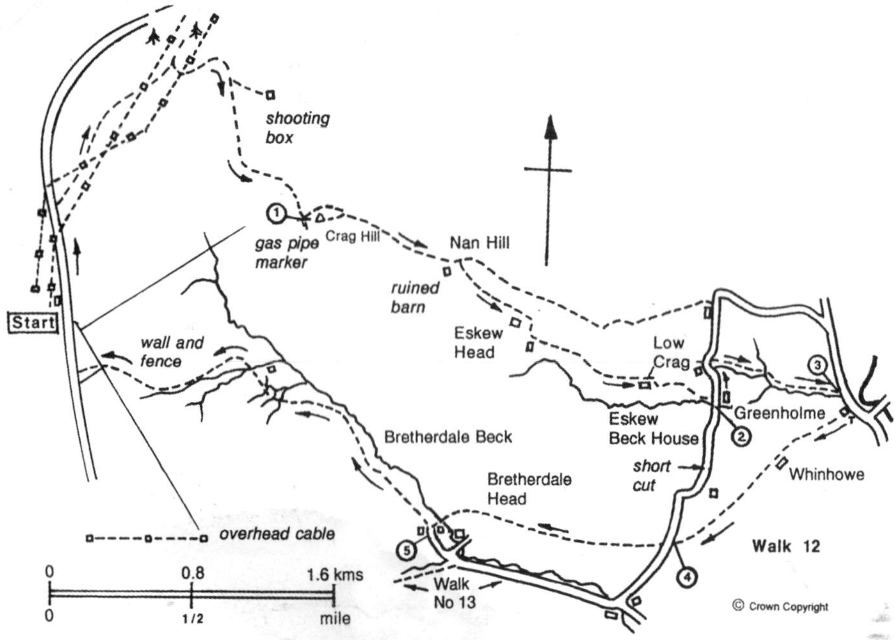
shooting box
gas pipe marker
Crag Hill
Nan Hill
ruined barn
Start
wall and fence
Eskew Head
Low Crag
Greenholme
Eskew Beck House
Bretherdale Beck
short cut
Whinhowe
Bretherdale Head
overhead cable
Walk 12
0
0.8
1.6 kms
0
1/2
mile
Walk No 13
© Crown Copyright

barn. Go through the gap above the barn, then contour across the next two fields above the marshes, ignoring a cart track cutting across diagonally, and keeping above the crags, to reach a wire fence with a stile at the intersection of another fence.

Cross the stile and continue to the converted farmhouse at Low Crag. Pass round to the left of the buildings and then pass a corrugated roofed building on your left, to find a stone stile in the corner of the wall at the end of the garden.

Contour across the fields keeping by the wall, then head downhill to a wooden stile at the junction of a wall and a fence. Follow the wall down to a gate and at its end and bear left across the field to a gate into a metalled lane at Eskew Beck House.

> (A short cut is possible here by following the road to the right for 750m to rejoin the main route where it crosses the road at the top of the hill. If doing this omit the next two paragraphs)

2. Turn left and follow the road for 220m to a footpath sign for Greenholme pointing down right to a stile at the wall corner near the small beck. Cross this stile and then another one ahead, then follow the wall and beck on the right

to a narrow gate at the bottom of the field. Cross the beck beyond the gate and follow it down through gorse bushes, crossing another stile and a second obscure wall stile in the corner of the wall to approach Greenholme. Just before the farm, cross a footbridge over the beck leading to a stile that brings you to the centre of the hamlet of Greenholme.

3.   Turn right and at the Village Hall with a red post box in the wall, turn immediately right where you see a finger post marked Bretherdale Head. Follow the track to Low Whinhowe a half ruined farmstead. Continue on through the farmyard but leave the track at a small group of outbuildings going straight ahead on a sunken track beside a wire fence. The sunken track is fairly clear on the ground and continues across several fields in the same direction, climbing gently for about 700m. It then descends slightly to join an unfenced metalled road near the top of a hill.

4. Cross the road. From here you can see down into the valley of Bretherdale which curves away to the right out of sight. Continue along the track that runs on the north side of the valley for 1000m.

Eventually the track descends towards Bretherdale Head where you cross Bretherdale beck by an unusual cantilevered stone footbridge.

BRETHERDALE BRIDGE   T. Baynes.

5.   After crossing the footbridge go right, alongside the beck, passing the next ruined building. Keep following the faint track, bearing left following the line of the river and going through a gate in a wire fence. The track continues, climbing gradually up the valley above the beck and crossing some very wet patches of ground, for another 600m until reaching another ruined wall. Don't go through the gateway, but follow the line of the sunken track up beside the wall, crossing three more tributaries of the main beck before the wall veers off right.

Now cross some open ground at the same level, still on a faint track, to reach a ford at the junction of two more tributaries. After this, keep ahead, up the line of rubble that marks the edge of the track. At the end of the stones the track curves to the left, but it disappears only to reappear 20m higher up the fell, going diagonally up the slope to the left. Keep climbing gently, parallel to the small beck on the left aiming for the dip in the skyline. When you reach a ditch draining into the nearby beck, before you reach the wall, turn 45 degrees right and aim for the highest ground ahead, to reach a wall just over the summit. Follow the wall right to a stile and gate. This leads across the heather to the stile and the A6. Turn right for 300m to reach the car park.

WALK NO. 13

Bretherdale and Borrowdale
15.4km (9.5miles)   1400ft of climb

The walk starts in the Borrowdale that crosses the A6. It visits the Bretherdale valley and combines some rough upland tracks with about two miles of little used country roads. After visiting the hamlet of Roundthwaite, close to the M6 motorway, the return route crosses the bracken clad slopes of Roundthwaite common, where navigation is not easy, before descending steeply into Borrowdale and returning along the valley floor.

Park in the lay-by just before Hucks Bridge about 7½ miles north of Kendal on the A6.   Map Ref: NY 552038.

OS map 1:25,000 OL7 North Sheet

Note the direction of North on the map.

Start
Walk down the road and just beyond Huck's Bridge go through the gate on the right and follow the river bank past two cross walls. Follow the path down to the river bank and opposite a gate overlooking the river take the bridleway which goes half left, steeply up the fell side. This is the Breasthigh road which is followed to the col. It then descends into the Bretherdale valley. On the descent take the route that crosses a tributary by a stone bridge and then follows close by the right-hand side of the main beck until it reaches the metalled drive to Bretherdale Head.

1. Turn right and continue alongside the beck on the metalled drive to reach a walled road at Midwath Stead. Turn right along the road for about 1.3km to Bretherdale Hall. 300m past Bretherdale Hall take a drive on the right, signed Dyke Farm. Follow the drive steeply up to Bretherdale Foot, a converted farmhouse. Turn sharp left in front of the house and walk straight ahead

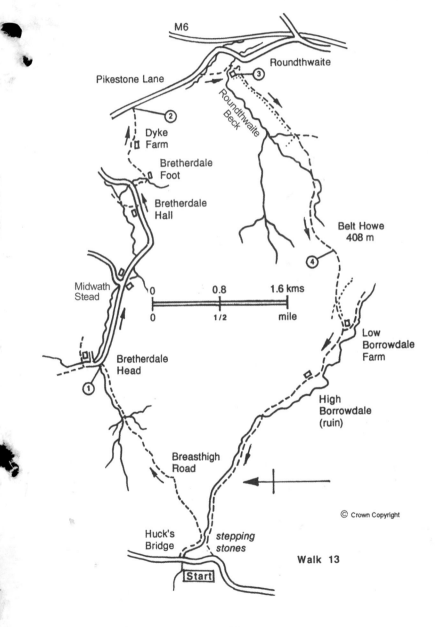

through a gate then a gap, into an open field, bear slightly left and down hill and follow a small stream on the right to a stile and footbridge.

Cross the bridge and go straight up the field to Dyke Farm, ahead, reaching the farmyard through the field gate just left of the house. Continue straight ahead along the farm drive to the road - Pikestone Lane. The farm drive is not a Right of Way but the owner has given permission to use it.

2. Turn right along the road, descending for about 1km. When a beck appears running alongside the road on the right, look for a signpost to Roundthwaite and a small gate. This leads to a footbridge. Cross the bridge and climb up the opposite bank to a gate into a field and diagonally across the field to walk between two walls. Go through the left hand gate facing you, and, keeping the wall on your right, descend to Barn End. Turn left along the drive to a stile on the right which leads down a small field to a footbridge over Roundthwaite Beck. After crossing the footbridge over Roundthwaite Beck turn right, then left, then right again, all in quick succession, and climb steeply up to gain the bridleway that starts alongside a wall on the right and leads up the fell to a gate in a fence.

3. Follow the intake wall on your right until it turns away sharply down the hill, then, ignoring a track that goes half left up the fell, continue straight ahead on the level, aiming for the right-hand side of a small valley ahead with bracken covered banks. Go above the bracken slope and over the low grassy hill to reach a wet patch of ground.

Cross this and after about another 150m follow the track as it swings left and climbs up to a small rock with stones on top which marks a junction of paths. Ignore the more distinct path straight ahead but turn sharp left just before this cairn on a feint path which rises right to another rock (with stones) and rises along the right side of a shallow valley with patches of rushes. This crosses the ridge at the col to the right of Belt Howe, the nearest high point on the ridge.

4. On reaching the top of the col the path becomes clearer and descends quite steeply to reach Low Borrowdale Farm. Do not go into the farmyard but continue on the cart track below the trees keeping right at a junction. The path soon becomes grassy and passes High Borrowdale Farm via gates. This farm is now owned by the Friends of the Lake District, where they are carrying out conservation and restoration work. Eventually you reach a bridge over the beck, and a hard track leads for a further mile to climb steeply back to the A6 and the start of the walk.

WALK NO. 14

Old Hutton and Millholme
14.5km (9miles)   Undulating

This walk is through gently undulating pastoral scenery, with many wild flowers in the lanes in spring and summer. In summer there are several fields ready for cutting for silage, so the walk is not recommended when the grass is long to avoid trampling the crop, an important part of the local economy. Maize may also be encountered.

The start of the walk is on the A65, about 4 miles south of Kendal. After 3½ miles note a turning to Halfpenny on the left. In a further half mile park in a lay-by. A finger post pointing into a wood, saying "Bridleway – Low Park Lane", indicates the start of this walk. Map ref: SD 536864.

OS map   1:25,000   OL7   South Sheet.

Note the direction of North on the map.

Start
From the lay-by follow the bridleway until it emerges into a field. Continue between the two mounds ahead, bearing slightly right and downhill to go through a small gate in the corner of the field, leading out onto a lane. Turn left along the road for a few metres and go up the drive of Low Park on the right, signposted Footpath to Holmescales.

Go straight through the garden, keeping to the right of a garden store, to a wooden stile over a low fence leading into a field. Continue by the boundary on the left until reaching Urchinrigg Farm, and go through a field gate on to the drive of the house. Keep round the right-hand side and along the back of the buildings, over the lawn, left of a row of cyprus trees and right of the greenhouse, to leave by another field gate to the north of the property. (This route is a diversion from the Right of Way, requested by the occupants but not yet official). Continue along the field with the hedge / wall on the right through two field gates, keeping in the same northerly direction to reach Peasey Beck on your right. Follow the beck upstream for about 500m, crossing a number of stiles, until reaching a footbridge.

Cross the bridge and go by the side of the wall along two fields to reach a road another 500m, opposite Homescale Activity Lodge.

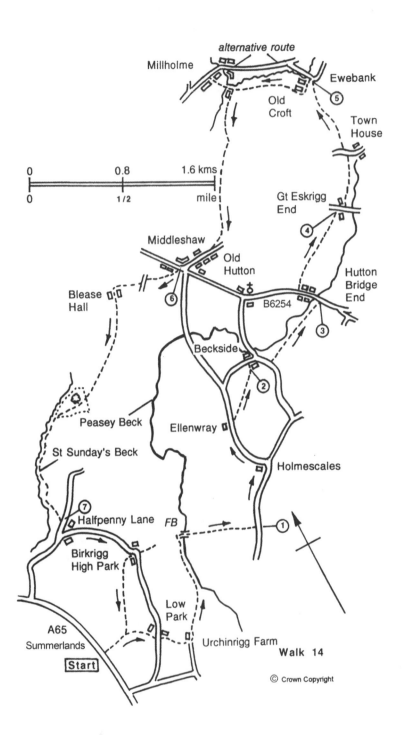

alternative route

Millholme

Ewebank

⑤

Old
Croft

Town
House

0   0.8   1.6 kms

0   1/2   mile

Gt Eskrigg
End

④

Middleshaw

Old
Hutton

Hutton
Bridge
End

Blease
Hall

⑥

B6254

③

Beckside

②

Peasey Beck

Ellenwray

St Sunday's Beck

Holmescales

⑦

Halfpenny Lane   *FB*

①

Birkrigg
High Park

A65
Summerlands

Low
Park

Urchinrigg Farm

Walk 14

[Start]

© Crown Copyright

46

1. Turn left and follow the road for about 700m, then turn left into Popplemire Lane just beyond Holmescales. Continue along the lane for another 600m to the next farm, Ellenwray. Go through the gate on the right, opposite the converted barn and head diagonally left across the field to a gate by a power line post. Now aim for the left of the buildings seen ahead, and emerge onto a road at Beckside by a field gate.

2. Turn right, and bearing right at the junction, follow the road for about 100m to a wall gap stile on the left in the corner of the field. Aim diagonally left across this rough pasture to where the wall on the right meets the ravine of Peasey Beck. Cross the wall by a ladder stile. This land is owned by the Woodland Trust. The walk continues through the open meadow, parallel to the beck. Continue over several stiles to reach the B6254 at Hutton Bridge End.

> (A short cut, reducing the walk by about 5 km, may be taken here by continuing along this road to the left for just under 1 km, as far as Middleshaw Bridge. Omit the next 3 paragraphs if doing this and go to para 6).

3. Turn left along the road for 250m to a footpath sign on the right, to Great Eskrigg End, one field beyond the last house. Go through the field gate and after 50m, go over a stile by a stone built sub-station on the right. Then follow the field boundary uphill to a wooden stile below a clump of trees. Keep by the trees on the left to another gate, then contour along the next field with a minor power line on your left, to a waymarked stile, in the stone wall. Continue by the boundary on the left across two more fields to reach Great Eskrigg End. Bear left between the converted farm-buildings to reach a road.

4. Turn right on the road to where, just past Great Eskrigg End House, a sign on the garage wall indicates the Public Right of Way. Go through an iron gate in the corner of the garage court and follow a gravel path through the garden to a small gate beside the shed, leading to a field. Bear right to a field gate, then aim uphill to another field-gate and a ladder stile seen ahead.

Continue along the next field, keeping by the hedge on the right, to reach the drive to Town House through a gate near a cattle grid. Cross the cattle grid and very soon, where the drive bears left, go diagonally off right, across the field to the right hand gate in the far corner.

Through the gate bear left between two pylons to another gate. Continue to a wooden stile then follow the same line to reach a gate at the bottom of the field, right of the converted farm buildings at Ewebank, and emerge onto another road.

5.   Bear left, following the Ewebank sign, and after a left-hand bend, follow a bridleway sign on the right to Old Croft. Keep left of the converted barn and along the back of it to reach a fenced path going into a narrow hedged lane. This is very wet underfoot and apt to be overgrown in summer, but it can be avoided by following the road through Millholme hamlet - see map. The hedged green lane continues for about 200m then opens into a field. Keep by the hedge on the right down to Old Croft Farm, passing through a field gate. Just before the barn turn left, then right, between the sheds. Turn left to a gate and stile into a field, and continue with the hedge on your right. Just before the end of the second field bear slightly left to a stile by a field gate. After crossing this continue straight ahead with a hedge on your right to a gate at the next bend. (A beef bull may be grazing with cows in this last field). Continue along the hedge on the right to the next field, and cross a stile and gate to follow the line of a former hedge on your left. Now keep straight ahead as far as a ladder stile under the first pylon line. Keep at the same level in the next field, cross a stile, keeping to the right of the post and wire fence, and continue to reach a gate. Then follow the old rutted track across the field towards the houses seen ahead. A rough track below the bungalow leads to a finger post and a narrow lane. Turn right along the lane past Middleshaw to reach the B6254 again at the northern end of Old Hutton village.

If you have decided to cut out the last three paragraphs rejoin the walk here.

6.   Virtually opposite the Middleshaw sign find a "Public Footpath" finger post. Follow this narrow path for 100m to a stile. Then with a hedge on your right keep along the right hand side of the field for a further 100m. At the opening turn right and strike straight uphill towards a power line post. Over the hill find a stone squeeze stile onto a green lane. Turn left for 20m to a wooden stile on the right. Then up and over the drumlin ahead keeping a hedge on your left. In the corner of the field find a small waymarked iron gate which leads into a bungalow garden.

Exit by a tall, narrow, solid wooden gate into the grounds of Blease Hall. This building dates from around 1600AD and is one of the finest old farmhouses in this area. Keep straight ahead across the drive and through some trees. Aim for the left end of a large shed and find a small gap stile onto a road.

Turn left and go through the long farmyard to leave it by a rough lane at the far end. Follow this track, bearing right along the wall on reaching a field. Pass through a gate and in the next field keep the field boundary on your left and pass through another gate. Beyond the gate bear half right across the field to

Blease Hall

find a small plank bridge and ladder stile over a watercourse at the right end of the facing wall. Keep straight ahead to a kissing gate. The castle like building on your right is a 'syphon well', associated with the aqueduct from Haweswater. Enter the wood ahead, where many young trees have been planted, and follow the broad track to an iron stile at the far side. After crossing the stile continue alongside St Sunday's Beck on the right for about 1 km. Cross a number of stiles and eventually emerging via a field gate onto a narrow lane at Halfpenny.

7. Turn right along the lane to the next junction, then turn left and follow another lane for 700m to reach Birkrigg High Park. Follow the road round past the main farmhouse and turn right at the signpost to Storth End, going between a modern shed and the horse-schooling yard. At the end of the sheds turn left, and then right, to reach an old bridleway. Follow this to the left, through the wood. On reaching a field keep by the wall on your left along two fields, bearing slightly right at the end of the second one to re-enter the bridleway where the walk started via a high step stile. Turn right for the starting point.

WALK NO. 15

Howgill Fells and Upper Lune Valley
16km (10miles)   2000ft of climb

The Howgill Fells, lying between the eastern Lakeland fells and the Yorkshire Dales and Pennines, form a compact mass of rounded hills separated by very steep-sided valleys. They give magnificent views of the neighbouring hills and the coastal area around Morecambe Bay. The dry and grassy hills make easy walking, but the absence of distinguishing landmarks and the general similarity of the ridges and valleys makes for demanding navigation in mist. This walk over the ridges facing southwest rises to a maximum height of 2200ft and is best attempted on a clear day. Most of this walk is on Access Land where 'Freedom to Roam' was achieved by the CROW Act in 2000.

The walk starts on the main Kendal to Sedbergh road (A684)
After crossing the single lane bridge over the Lune, called Lincoln's Inn Bridge, continue for 300m and park in a lay-by beside the old St Gregory's Church on the right-hand side of the road. The start is also on the route of the Kendal to Sedbergh bus service. Map ref: SD 634922.

OS map 1:25,000   OL19   Howgill Fells.

Start
Walk along the road towards Sedbergh and take the first road on the left, Slacks Lane. After a few metres turn right up the drive to the buildings of Underwinder. Go to the right of Greenmantle, a converted barn, then continue through a gate and up, to cross a stile into a field. Keep by the left-hand boundary of two fields to reach Howgill Lane. Turn left along the road for 400m to a signpost on the right to Brant Fell; this enclosed track leads to the open fell via a gate. Go right then left up the fell aiming for the high ground ahead, and before long you should join a good track that leads direct to the summit of Winder with its trig point at 473m (1551ft).

1.   From the trig point on a clear day the route ahead is plainly visible, climbing over the shoulder of Arrant Haw. Follow the well-trodden path, bearing right at a fork. (A detour is possible to the top of Arrant Haw, rejoining the main route further on).

Drop down after Arrant Haw and then climb steeply beside a wire fence to the top of Calders.

At the summit, which is marked by a low cairn, leave the wire fence on the right and turn left to join another clear track that can be seen ahead, over Bram Rigg rising to the trig point at the top of the Calf, the highest point in the Howgills at 676m (2220ft).

2. From the Calf veer slightly left in a north-westerly direction (ignoring the track going off right) to pick up a clear track that follows the ridge of White Fell round to the left in a gentle curve. Soon the track descends quite steeply and in about 2km you reach a ford (hopefully not too deep) at the confluence of Calf beck and Long Rigg beck.

Continue along the track over the left flank of Castley Knott to reach a walled lane by a gate just above some sheep pens, that leads to Castley Farm. At the farm follow the sign to Gate Side, left, down the farm drive. Bear right past the farmhouse, and right again to enter a field through a gate. Continue along the track across the field to another gate and go up to a gap in the next wall and a sign pointing right to a ladder stile. From the stile go straight across the field

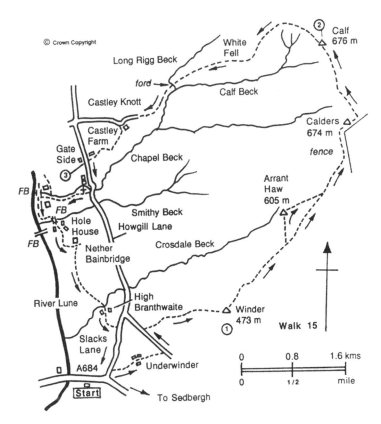

51

to join a track going left towards Gate Side. After a gate, keep round the left of the buildings to a stile out onto Howgill Lane (an old Roman road).

You could follow the Roman road left for just over 3km, all the way back to Slacks Lane, near the start. But a more interesting and slightly longer route follows the Chapel Beck bank and the Lune for a short distance on field paths. After the long sweeping sections on the Howgills, the following section is more detailed.

3. Go left along the lane for 400m, but immediately after crossing the bridge over Chapel Beck go through a gate on the right and down the road past Howgill Church and some converted mill buildings. Keep right at the fork and continue by the beck, leaving the road immediately before it crosses a bridge to Beckside Farm. Go left onto a grassy track beside the beck. Follow the beck, passing through a gate, to where it joins the River Lune near a footbridge. This is the Dales Way long distance path. Don't cross the bridge but turn left and follow the riverbank round to where a fence blocks your way. Go left and follow the fence and cross a stile in the next corner, then follow the beckside path up to a footbridge. Cross the bridge and go straight ahead between the buildings of Hole House and through the gated farmyards.

At the top of the yards, after the third gate, is a signpost. Closely follow the direction of the signpost over the knoll, to reach the right hand of two gates in the wall where it meets a fence. Follow the left-hand wall to a signpost at the next farm, Nether Bainbridge. Turn right in front of the buildings, but soon turn left over a wall stile and turn right into a lane. Follow this, keeping in the same direction past a small barn.

Continue uphill gradually nearing the overhead wires, to cross a stile in a wall corner near an electricity pole. Continue by the left-hand field boundary to another wall stile. Cross the field to a gate just left of a hen house. The Dales Way is left behind at this point.

Go through the gate and follow the boundary to the left of the buildings, reaching an enclosed track.

Follow the right hand wall to another footbridge, leading over Crosdale Beck to High Branthwaite. Go through the farmyard, leaving by the gate ahead, then, after a few paces, bear left at a junction and enter a field by a gate. Cross the field by the wall on the left to a wooden stile in the corner. Now go half left over a ruined wall and straight up the hill to reach Slacks Lane again by a gated stone wall at the top of the field to the left of the wood. Turn right for 800m down the road to the starting point.

WALK NO. 16
Middleton Fell and the Lune Valley
21km (13miles)   2000ft of climb

This varied walk involves a fairly strenuous climb up to a maximum height of 609m (1997ft) from where you are rewarded by splendid all round views. There is a good long ridge walk and a pleasant return through the pastures of the Lune valley. Choose a clear day, not only to get the best views but also because the path along the ridge is difficult to follow in mist, before the security of a guiding wall is reached. There are few landmarks. Remember it will be considerably colder on top.

The start of the walk is in Barbon. Turn right off the A683 about 2 miles north of Kirkby Lonsdale. Park near the church.   Map Reference SD 631824

OS 1:50,000 Land Ranger 97.   OS 1:25,000 Explorer OL2, West Sheet

Start
Take the road to the right of the church to the Manor. Cross the cattle grid and bridge over Barbon Beck. After about 120m leave the road at the right-hand bend, to head straight across the park towards the right-hand side of the wood ahead. Keep the wood on your left to reach a gate into a field before Eskholme Farm.

Continue along the bottom of the field towards the farm and then turn right, up the field to another gate near some mature trees.

Climb steeply up the fell, getting gradually closer to a wall on the right, to cross some crags and reach the cairn at Eskholme Pike (307m). Follow the clear path up the ridge, bearing left away from the wall in about 700m. Climb steadily for about 1.5km, pass another small cairn, to reach a large cairn on Castle Knott (536m).

The path now dips down over wetter ground before rising again. Aim for the corner of a wall coming in from the right (the boundary of the Yorkshire Dales National Park). Continue along by the wall to reach the trig point on Calf Top at 609m (1999ft) (a different one to the highest point in the Howgills).

From here on a clear day the view takes in Ingleborough (SE), the Forest of Bowland, Morecambe Bay and the Lancashire Coast to the South. The Furness peninsular lies to the SW and a panorama of the Lakeland fells is

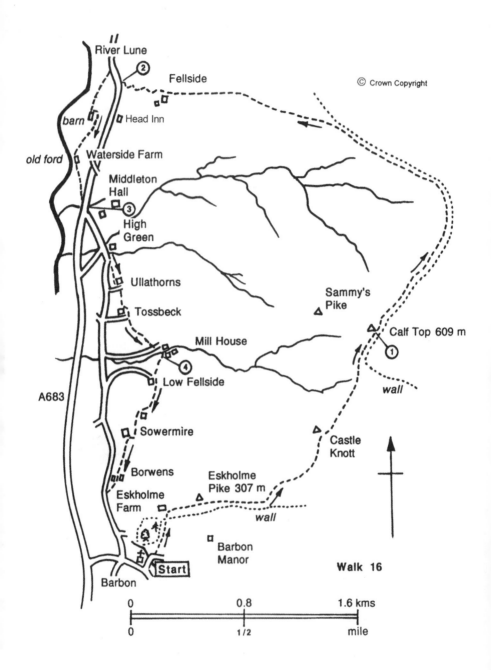

River Lune
②
Fellside
© Crown Copyright
barn
Head Inn
old ford
Waterside Farm
Middleton Hall
③
High Green
Ullathorns
Sammy's Pike △
Tossbeck
Calf Top 609 m △
①
Mill House
④
Low Fellside
wall
A683
Sowermire
Castle Knott △
Borwens
Eskholme Pike 307 m △
Eskholme Farm
wall
Barbon Manor
Walk 16
Start
Barbon

| 0 | | 0.8 | | 1.6 kms |
| 0 | | 1/2 | | mile |

seen to the West, going round to the Howgills in the North with Sedbergh town nestling below them. Dentdale lies to the NE.

1. From Calf Top continue alongside the wall on the right for about 3.5km (2.25miles), pass a stone grouse butt and in 350m keep left at a path junction, leaving the wall. Follow the main path downhill, ignoring minor tracks to left and right. After 800m pass to the right of a wall, cross several fords over small becks and in a further 1.5km you reach Fellside Farm. From here the farm drive descends to the main road through a delightful nature reserve with many flowers in spring and summer.

2. The Head Inn, serving bar food, is now about 400m to the left should you require refreshments, but otherwise turn right along the A683 for 150m. Keep left at a road junction and in 50m go through a gate on the left and through a wood on a track leading down to the River Lune. Just before reaching a gate into a field bear left and continue along the bottom of the wood to another gate into a field. Go along the bottom of the field then bear right towards a barn. Go through the gate left of the barn and keep by the hedge on the left until approaching Waterside Farm, then go down a small path to the riverbank, the site of a former ford, and climb up behind the farmhouse to a gate into the yard.

Continuing in the same southerly direction going through a gate into a fenced track, at the end of which you take the right-hand of two gates, leading into a field. Continue by the fence/hedge on the left passing through two gates, reaching a large open field.

Cross this to the far left-hand corner, where a gate gives access to the A683 again, opposite the drive to Middleton Hall, a fine example of a 15th Century fortified farmhouse.

3. Take the minor road, signposted High Green, beside the entrance to the farm. From here it is possible to follow this very quiet road for about 5km all the way back to the starting point at Barbon.

This may be desirable at times when the fields are full of long grass. However, for a more adventurous and slightly longer route, involving a little climbing, follow the minor road for approx. 800m.

Then, 220m after crossing the beck, ignore a minor road on the right, and go through a stile on the left at the right-hand bend in the road, leading straight ahead into a field.

oss the field, aiming towards Ullathorns seen ahead. Go through the right-and gate in the corner of the field and another gate, leading into the yard in front of the farmhouse. Turn right between the buildings and go through the right-hand gateway leading to the farm drive. Now go through another gate straight ahead leading into a field and follow the wall on the left until it turns away at a corner. Bear half left towards the next farm, Tossbeck, entering the yard by a field gate.

Turn left in front of the gable end of the farmhouse and go up the yard to an archway under the old railway line. On emerging from the underpass cross a concrete slab bridge, and then keep right, parallel to the old railway to find a stile in the next wall. Cross the track to a second stile 10m to the left. Cross the field to another wall stile, then go down to a gate and stile in the left-hand corner of the next field, bearing sharp left to the next stile. Now go diagonally right to a stile in the internal corner of the next wall, and having crossed this continue on the same line towards the trees over the brow of the hill, to reach a stile and gateway 20m left of a large tree. Still on the same line, aim for a stile at the junction of wall and fence ahead, leading to the Mill House road. Go up the road to the farm ahead through a gate to Mill House Cottages.

Turn right before the last pair of cottages to find a stile leading to a bridge over the beck.

4. After crossing the beck at Mill House go through the gate 25m to the right of the barn ahead, then turn half right and make a beeline for the roofs, once you can see them over the brow of the hill in front.

On reaching this farm, Low Fellside, cross a wall stile into a horse paddock. Keep left of the buildings to a field gate, continue past an old barn on the right to a small gate, turn right to go through a third gate, then turn left. Keep along the bottom of two fields and round the left and far sides of the third to pass another barn. Go through the gate in the corner of the field, and follow the stony track to where it goes alongside the old railway embankment to reach Sowermire through an archway.

Bear left in front of the farmhouse. Follow the drive down for about 70m to cross a stile on the left at the corner of a wood. Cross the small footbridge over the beck, then aim between the two large trees seen ahead to a gap in a ruined wall. After this veer left towards the next and last farm, Borwens. Pass in front of the farmhouse and bear right through a gate at the end of the yard to cross a small field diagonally to a stile onto a minor road. Follow this road left for about 1 km back to Barbon.

WALK NO. 17

Longsleddale
20km, 12.5miles or 7.5km or 4.6 miles   1600ft of climb in total

The valley of Longsleddale, north of Kendal, is an area of great beauty in the Lake District National Park, and still relatively unfrequented by walkers. The lush green pastures in the valley bottoms are 'in-bye' grazing for numerous sheep and cattle. Please take special care to control dogs and leave gates as found. The longer walk also includes stretches of wild and desolate moorland to the west of the valley. This is not country to venture into when there is mist, as there are many boggy areas and the tracks are not clear in places.

However, it can be a rewarding walk at all times of the year, not least when the heather is in bloom in August.

From Kendal travel north on the A6 for about 4 miles. Go past the turning to Longsleddale for about 2/3 mile and look for an electricity sub-station on the left. Turn here and park in an small lay-by just past a turning on the left. Much of the walk is on bridleways that are quite well waymarked by blue arrows on a yellow background.   Map Reference: SD 530999.

O S map 1:25,000 OL7   Northern Sheet

Start
Walk back 50m and turn right to Mosergh Farm. Just before the farm turn right onto a walled bridleway and follow it towards the prominent cairned peak of Whiteside Pike for 630m, passing a walled track on the right before reaching another bridleway sign on the left.

Turn left here through the gate and follow the track until it opens into a field, here maintaining height by bearing right, where two marker posts show the way ahead. Beyond the second post, drop down steeply left, aiming for a gate in the wall ahead where it reaches a small plantation. Pass through this gate, over a small stream and alongside the wood to merge, 60m beyond it, with a cart track traversing the hillside on the right. Continue the long quite steep descent down this bridleway to arrive at the Longsleddale valley road, via Murthwaite Farm.

1. Turn right along the road for 570m, passing Low House drive on the right. Take note of this, as it will be a useful marker to aim for on the return route,

hen you cross the moorland on the other side of the valley. Continue a further 430m along the road before turning left onto a bridleway to cross the bridge over the River Sprint on the access road to Docker Nook farm. A Right of Way turns off to the left 50m beyond the bridge. At this point the short and long walks divide; if doing the longer walk continue straight on, omitting the next paragraph.

THE SHORTER WALK

2. Cross the footbridge over Dockernook Gill and pass through the gate on the left. Aim straight across the field for the white farmhouse seen ahead, coming close to the Sprint before passing through a gate onto a good track that rises to the farm, Bridge End. This makes a walk of 4.75 miles. To continue go to paragraph 8.

THE LONGER WALK

2. Proceed towards Docker Nook farm and, 40m beyond the first gate, turn sharp right at a finger post marking a junction of bridleways. Go through the right-hand of two gates seen ahead, and follow the green track beside the wire fence. The route is easy to follow as it passes through gates with the wall / fence on one side, then on the other.

Continue straight ahead at Kilnstones, passing through the gate at the end of the barn on the right and over the footbridge just beyond. The accompanying wall / fence continues up the slope on the left and two more waymarked gates show the route towards the next dwelling, Beech Hill.

With the wall now on your right, continue past Beech Hill, noting Longsleddale's church across the river. Go through the small gate ahead, and then bear 45 degrees right, as waymarked, dropping steeply down towards the beck (NOT to the wall gap just ahead) to a further waymark post near the wall corner.

3. Walk away from Beech Hill, with the wall on your left to another gate. Cross the middle of the next four fields and through a gate into an enclosed lane leading to the farmyard at Wad's Howe. Here the route is clearly waymarked, go diagonally right across the yard and through a small gate at the left side of a long barn. It leads, beside the barn, to a wicket gate through which the path now turns sharp left to follow alongside the wall, eventually crossing two streams and through a gate to approach the next dwelling, Hollin Root. Just before the gate into the yard, turn up left to a field gate onto an enclosed lane which leaves the valley and ascends to a large tract of rough moorland (now Access Land).

4. The broad stony track winds up the hillside for 560m, reaching open country at a gate near a ruined building. Continue ahead close to the wall on your left eventually passing through a wire fence via a kissing gate giving access to the open moor. Initially keep near the wall but, where it bends left, avoid the worst bogs by veering slightly right to cross a line of stone grouse butts and reach a waymark post just over a slight rise. From here the track resumes its generally westerly course and the undulating, meandering route is relatively easy to follow. Soon Skeggles Water can be seen over on the right and the track attains its maximum elevation (324m) before swinging right to reach a gate in the wall marking the western boundary of Longsleddale parish.

5. The rough moorland continues as the path gradually descends to cross Skeggleswater Dyke, the stream that flows from the tarn to join the Kent just north of Staveley. Ahead is a second wall where the heather moorland is left via a gate giving access to rough pasture and bracken slopes; green fields lie ahead. A small cairn near a ruined barn marks the junction with a bridleway coming down from Green Quarter Fell above Kentmere.

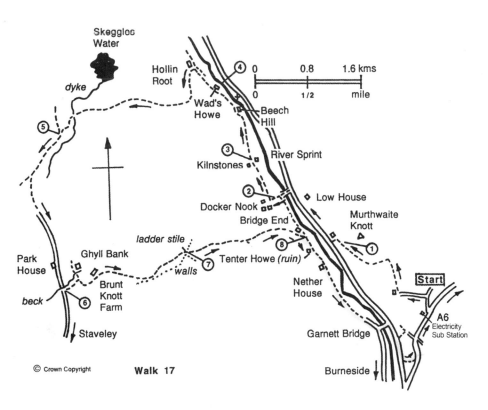

© Crown Copyright   **Walk 17**

59

As the track snakes away southwards, the upper reaches of Morecambe Bay can be seen in the distance, while the Kentmere valley lies over on the right.

Through the next gateway the gradient eases and at a further gate the bridleway becomes a byway open to all traffic. At the large complex of Park House the track becomes a tarmac road. Continue ahead gently downhill for another 750m where, at an S bend, the road goes over a beck and immediately beyond it a footpath sign points left over a stile.

6.   Go uphill beside the beck, crossing two stiles, as they come into view. Reach the access lane to Upper High House, below the large white house, Ghyll Bank. Turn right and cross the cattle grid, continuing along the road and over another cattle grid. Now turn sharp left, up the drive to Brunt Knott Farm.

Go up between the buildings, through two gates, and wind uphill on the cart track to climb a ladder stile by the next gate. Now follow the clear path climbing steadily, quite close to a wire fence on the right. As the gradient eases, a stone wall on the right is approached; ignore the metal gate and step stile at either side of its junction with another wall. Instead, continue uphill on the clear track which curves slightly left where the main wall disappears into

River Sprint from Garnet Bridge

the waters of a tiny tarn. Just ahead, the highest point of the pass (and of the whole walk) at 365m is reached. Keep ahead at a right fork in the path and soon a stile in a wire fence shows the way forward. Skirt left round the next marshy patch and, keeping to the base of the steeper ground on the left, follow the white waymarked route until opposite a prominent ladder stile in the wall on the right. Now drop down to reach the stile.

7. Once over the ladder stile bear half left to follow a fairly distinct track going along a low ridge between two watercourses, before crossing that on the right, as well as several other tributaries of Dockernook Gill, which soon becomes dominant on the left. Always keeping well above the main gill, continue ahead, noting the point where you are in line with the first wall descending the opposite side of the valley. About 160m ahead is a key junction. Take the left fork where the path bends slightly right.

Now descend steadily on a clear track, aiming towards Low House Farm (passed on the outward route) seen ahead across the Longsleddale valley. Follow the track down to Bridge End. Turn right through the gate onto the farm drive.

8. Continue on the track past Tenter Howe (ruined) and then 600m to Nether House farm. Look for a slate sign on the wall that indicates that the path goes through the gate on the right. It continues alongside the beck to reach a field. Go by the wall on your right and take the right-hand of two gates into the next field. Note the waymark and cross the middle of the next field to the gate at its far right-hand corner.

Pass through and continue ahead, descending left of the line of trees before curving left, then right, round a large pond to pass the end of the drive to Cocks Close on your left. Continue ahead, swinging left then right and climbing slightly, now with the wall / fence on your left. Take a gate on the left into an enclosed green lane leading down to the hamlet of Garnett Bridge. Cross the bridge and turn right up the hill for 160m. Turn left into a bridleway climbing steadily for 250m before turning right at a T junction to reach the A6. Turn left along the A6 for 480m to the electricity sub station and turn left to where your car is parked.

WALK NO. 18

Kirkby Lonsdale to Kendal

24 km (15 miles) or two halves of about 7½ miles. **Undulating**

This walk, satisfyingly linking the two towns, follows quiet lanes, field paths, ancient bridleways, the old canal towpath and riverside paths. The walk is best done by taking the bus from Kendal to Kirkby Lonsdale and walking back. The bus passes the Crooklands Hotel, where the walk could be divided into two. Go to paragraph 7 for the walk from Crooklands to Kendal.

O S 1:25,000 OL 2 West Sheet OL 7 South Sheet OL 7 North Sheet

Start
From Kirkby Lonsdale Market Square, go up New Road from the right-hand corner of the Square. On reaching a T-junction (road sign 'Mitchelgate' opposite) turn left and shortly fork left, signed as a cul-de-sac. At the A65, cross, and continue ahead up the road signed to Burton and Hutton Roof.

1. After about 200m, turn right through a metal gate, signed "Footpath to High Biggins". Follow the clear path up to the top of the field, then through woodland, to emerge on a road. Turn right, initially between a few houses, for 400m to where a stony track turns off left. In the angle between this track and the road, go through a squeeze stile into the field.

Cross the field diagonally and go through a stile on the opposite side, which may not be visible until you are close to it. Go round animal pens, then continue rather to the right of your previous direction, but bearing a little to the left from the right-hand field edge. You should be heading roughly towards the right-hand side of the low, rocky hill visible in the distance if it's clear. In the wall, once visible, go through a stile.

Continue along the rocky crest of the next field, roughly equidistant between its right and left edges, to a gate and an inadequate stile in the far wall. Beyond the gate, the path divides.

Your route keeps along the right-hand field wall. Continue in this direction across three further fields. In the third field, where the right-hand wall turns away right, continue still in the same direction to a gate in the far wall. To the right of the gate, go through a stile on to a road. Cross, and go through a gate signed "Bridleway to Hollin Hall and Sealford".

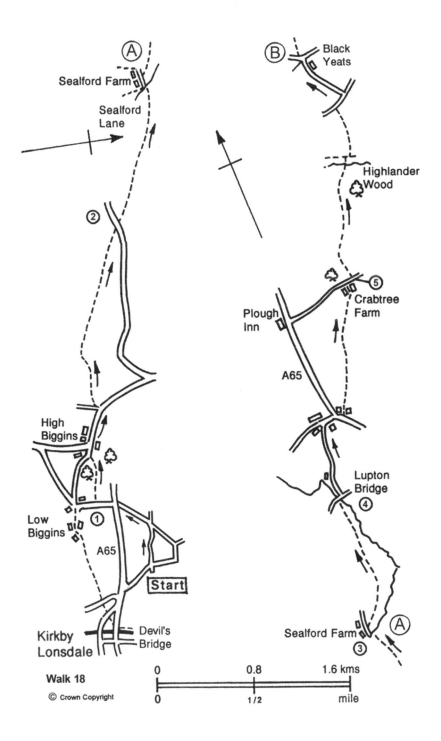

Walk 18

© Crown Copyright

2. Go immediately past animal pens and through another gate Then bear left onto a bridleway, passing to the right of the ancient settlement Kilnerfoot, to a marker post showing the crossing paths. Follow the blue bridleway arrow to a gate.

Continue across the next field still in the same direction, heading towards the right-hand side of the buildings of Sealford Farm, now visible 750m ahead, to reach a gate into the enclosed Sealford Lane For much of its length this may be muddy or overgrown, but at the farm it becomes tarmaced. A few metres beyond the farm, cross a stile to the right, signposted "Public Footpath Lupton Bridge".

3. The path sets off obliquely to the line of the road, then curves progressively leftward, following the contour of the hill, to reach a fence crossed by a double stile. Avoid descending rightward towards the valley bottom, cross the double stile, and continue in the same direction of the waymarked arrow, still bearing a little to the left and now climbing slightly, to reach a wire fence which climbs from the valley bottom. Climb with this fence on your right to cross a stile in the corner of the field.

In the next field, which can be wet and rushy in places, continue in roughly your previous direction, bearing downhill, leaving on your left the hedge which runs along the top of the field. When the hedge on the far side comes into view, head roughly half way down it. Look for and cross double stiles into the next field.

Bear only slightly to the right, heading towards the right-hand side of the buildings of Badger Gate visible 750m ahead. Go through a waymarked gate in the further fence, and continue ahead to reach an electricity pole next to the bank of the main stream, Lupton Beck. Continue on, crossing a footbridge over a shallow ditch, then joining a track beside a fence. Follow this to the right, then through a metal gate into a yard area with the farm above to the left. Cross the yard to a wall stile on to a road.

4. Turn right for 750m along a road to a T-junction, then right to reach the main A65. Here you need to cross into the gap between the second (Smithy Cottage) and third buildings opposite, counting from the left. Once there, with your back to the main road, turn left into a fenced gravel path along the back of the houses, signed to Crabtree. Cross a parking area and continue into the field ahead, the A65 now being away to your left.

At the far right corner of the field, go through a gate into the next field. Bear away from the left-hand hedge, uphill, heading for a gate which becomes visible in the far corner. To the left of the gate, cross a small footbridge and stile into the next field. Bear right, close to but above the right-hand fence.

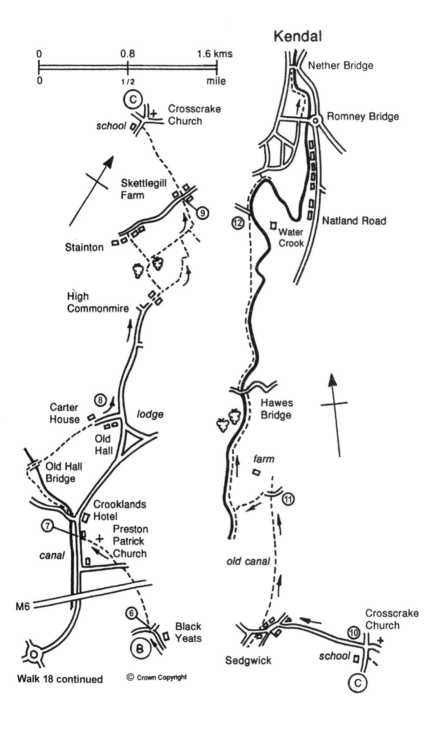

Kendal

Nether Bridge

Romney Bridge

Natland Road

Crosscrake Church

school

ⓒ

Water Crook

⑫

Skettlegill Farm

⑨

Stainton

High Commonmire

Hawes Bridge

farm

⑪

Carter House

⑧

lodge

Old Hall

Old Hall Bridge

Crooklands Hotel

Preston Patrick Church

⑦

canal

old canal

M6

⑥

Black Yeats

Ⓑ

Sedgwick

Crosscrake Church

⑩

school

ⓒ

Walk 18 continued

© Crown Copyright

0   0.8   1.6 kms

0   1/2   mile

Continue in this direction, passing through a gate, above a small wooded valley to the right. Crabtree Farm shortly becomes visible ahead.

On reaching a hedge, go right a few metres on a track, then left through a gate and along a stony track. Continue through the farm buildings to reach double gates on to Crabtree Lane. Turn right, signposted to Lupton High, past a "Private Road No Entry" sign. After 100m, turn left through the first gate on the left.

5. Follow the left-hand field edge, bearing right and uphill at the corner, and go through a gate to the left. Continue along left-hand field edges to enter the bottom of Highlander Wood. Keep along the bottom of the wood until you reach a waymarked post, where diverge from the wood, diagonally across the field to its far corner. This can be wet, so it's better to stay a little up to the right.

Go down the steep bank, cross the stream, up the other side, and after a few metres go through a gate to the right. Go left on the track, downhill to reach a narrow road. Turn right and after 150m turn left on another road. Follow this for nearly 500m, past Black Yeats Farm, to a left bend where ahead are two gates. Cross a stile by the right-hand gate, signed to Crooklands.

6. Follow the left-hand field edge. Cross a further narrow field, then go through the tunnel below the M6 motorway. Go through a gate and turn immediately left through a second gate, then turn right and, with your back to the motorway, cross the field towards the large stone house ahead, diverging a little from the hedge on the right. Cross two stiles separated by a stone footbridge. Turn left on the road for a few metres.

Beyond the drive entrance, turn right through a wicket gate and go up the right-hand field edge. Go through a second wicket gate into Preston Patrick Churchyard, then on as before with the wall now on your left. Leave the churchyard at its further corner, and continue down a clear path to the A65. Turn right for about 200m, and then left on the B6385, signed to Milnthorpe. The Crooklands Hotel is a few metres further along the A65 should you wish refreshments. If the walk is being done in two halves a bus can be caught here back to Kendal.

7. Leave the road down steps by a low stone building on the right. Turn left on the canal towpath past the building, a base of the Canal Trust. After nearly ½ km, go up steps and across the bridge. With your back to the canal, continue along left-hand field edges. Pass to the left of a barn, through the stockyard, and bear a little to the right into a broad walled track.

8. Keep straight ahead through the buildings of Carter House farm. At a

T-junction, turn left on another enclosed lane, which leads after 1 km to High Commonmire Farm. Bear slightly right across the front of a range of barns on the right, to reach a gate and stile leading into a narrow, enclosed, unsurfaced lane which may be muddy. Beyond power lines, where a gate ahead leads into a field, go sharply left.

On reaching a T-junction, turn right on a broad hedged track. Where this turns right towards houses, continue in your previous direction across a stile into the field. Strictly, the right of way continues ahead for 100m, then turns directly left, as indicated by a waymark on a gatepost. But a trodden path, visible running diagonally down the field from the stile, indicates that in practice this is the way generally followed.

Either way, a stile soon becomes visible in the bottom wall. Cross, and climb diagonally up to reach at the crest of the hill a stile in the right-hand fence. Continue in the same line down the next field, through a gate at the left of the nearest barn of Skettlegill Farm, and down to the road.

9. Cross diagonally left, then cross a high stile into a builder's yard. Go to the right behind stone buildings to find a gate on the left. Cross the beck by a bridge, and climb directly up the hill to reach an angle in the fence which runs along the crest of the hill from the right.

Go downhill with the fence on your right, and cross a ladder stile in the bottom corner. Go diagonally to the right in the next field, then continue with the hedge on your right to a gate and stile in the field corner. Cross the next field diagonally to a gate in the middle of the opposite hedge, and turn right along the road to the crossroads. To the right is Crosscrake Church.

10. Turn left, signposted to Sedgwick. At the T-junction in the village, turn left, signposted to Hincaster and Milnthorpe. Immediately beyond the tunnel under the canal, turn right up the steps to the empty canal. Turn left along the towpath, following it through gates and fields, under a now isolated bridge, and through Larkrigg Wood.

11. 200m beyond the wood, turn left through a squeeze stile just before Larkrigg Hall Bridge. With your back to the canal, bear left down the steep bank, so you are heading obliquely back relative to your previous direction along the towpath. Continue in this diagonal direction to reach a gate in the far left corner of the field.

Follow this track beyond the gate, soon bending sharply left. After about 100m further, where on the left is a waymarked post, turn sharp right through a stone

Last lap. River Kent, about 1 mile South of Kendal

stile. Follow the obvious path above the river Kent, through woodland and then fields, until a stile leads left on to a road.

Cross Hawes bridge and go right for 50m. Where the road bends left, cross a stile on the right signposted to Scroggs Lane. The generally clear path follows right-hand field edges above the river until, in the sixth field from the road, it bears left, heading past a power line pole. Drop down to a footbridge over a small stream, climb over a flood bank, and continue through a long field to reach a gate with a gated stile to its left leading on to a road.

12. Cross obliquely, then, as the road bends left, continue above the river along a clear, broad path through a narrow belt of woodland. On reaching a T-junction of paths, go left between houses on to a residential road.

Turn right, and after 100m turn right again, Wattsfield Road. After 70 metres bear right, still Wattsfield Road. Continue ahead, rejoining the river, cross the main road into Romney Gardens, and turn immediately right on the tarmac footpath in front of the houses. Follow the path as it turns left, and continue with the river to the right. On reaching the main road, bear right and follow it for 750m to Kendal town centre. Alternatively, once past the bridge, turn right along the riverside walk to the town centre area.